LOST AND FOUND

LOST AND FOUND

The Search for my Family

Stephen A. Richardson

The Book Guild Ltd
Sussex, England

First published in Great Britain in 2001 by
The Book Guild Ltd
25 High Street
Lewes, East Sussex
BN7 2LU

Typesetting in Times by
Acorn Bookwork, Salisbury, Wiltshire

Printed in Great Britain by
Bookcraft (Bath) Ltd, Avon

A catalogue record for this book is available from
The British Library.

ISBN 1 85776 513 3

CONTENTS

1

Early Information About My Adoption

As long as I can remember, I have known that I was adopted, as were my older brother and younger sister. It did not seem to bother us, and I do not remember being curious about who my biological parents were, or the reasons why I was put up for adoption. I did know that the reason that my adoptive parents chose us was that they wanted children, but their blood types were incompatible, and that this had led to my adopted mother having a series of miscarriages. It was only later that I came to realize that being adopted did have effects on how I thought and what I did.

I remember when I was seven years old, going with my adoptive father and brother to a local police station for some purpose of registration. Much later I found out that this was done to comply with an adoption law that was passed in 1927.

Until I was nine we lived in a suburb of London, and then we moved to Paisley, Scotland, where my adoptive father became the head of the Paisley Technical College. After the move I experienced various forms of lung trouble and missed a lot of school through being ill. In hopes of getting over the problem, my adoptive parents decided that I should go to my mother's parents and her sister, Hilda, my adoptive grandparents and aunt, who lived in a seaside house in the Isle of Wight, where the climate was warmer and there was less rainfall. My grandparents were retired and my aunt, who had never married, helped take care of the household and carried on a voluminous correspondence with her nephews and nieces, who were all devoted to her. The house where I stayed was separated from the sea by a large stone wall. It was the heyday of the great Atlantic passenger ships, and we used to watch them slowly making their way up and down the Solent on their way to Southampton. To reach Seaview, the nearest village, we could walk along the beach, and I often accompanied Aunt Hilda when she went shopping. On one of these walks, she told me the following story about my biological parents and the circumstances of my adoption:

My mother was the daughter of a titled Catholic family in Yorkshire. She fell in love with the family chauffeur, and I was the result of the relationship. My birth mother put me up for adoption and asked the adoption agency to find a Catholic family who would take me. They were unable to find such a family, and when a Quaker family wanted to adopt me the agency accepted their request.

I do not know how much I thought about what Aunt Hilda told me, but I never forgot what she said. My adoptive parents were very good to me, and I was afraid that if I began asking them questions about my adoption they might interpret the questions as meaning that I did not fully accept them as my parents and might be hurt by my questioning. For this reason, I did not pursue any inquiries with them.

There were some ways in which knowing that I was adopted affected me. I always had a fantasy picture of my birth mother. I saw her as a young and beautiful woman who was all-loving and caring and an ideal mother. At times when I thought that my adoptive mother had been unkind or unjust, I would say to myself, 'If you had been my real mother, you would not have done that.' Somehow, this was very comforting.

It was not until I was grown up that I realized the ways in which eugenics theory had influenced our upbringing. Eugenics was based on the belief that genetic inheritance was the primary determinant of a person's intelligence and other characteristics, and this led some to advocate selective breeding in order to improve the quality of a population. The theory was first developed by Francis Galton in 1883. Galton left funds in his will for the establishment of a Chair of Eugenics at the University of London, and a famous statistician, Carl Pearson, became the first professor to hold this position. Before my birth, my adoptive father, who was a scientist and mathematician, worked for Pearson in 1907 and became interested in the relative roles that nature and nurture play in the development of intelligence in children. Eugenic theory played down the role of nurture or the social environmental influences on the development of children. For my adoptive father, the relative importance of nature and nurture was an issue for careful research, and he published a paper in the *Eugenics Review*, proposing a study that would include adopted children. Shortly afterwards, he shifted his research to meteorology.

Oliver Ashford, in a biography of my adoptive father, wrote, 'The main reasons [for their deciding to adopt children] were doubtless their love of youngsters and their desire to help children without a home or parents...' It has also been suggested that my adoptive father was keen to learn about the reaction of children to a caring and relatively affluent home environment. If, by good chance, he and his wife ever had children, he might even be able to contribute to the nature-nurture study that he had proposed earlier to the Eugenics Society.

Both my adoptive father and mother were very intelligent and came from families where members had achieved distinction at universities and in various professions. It was natural, then, that they hoped that their children would continue this tradition of intellectual ability, even though we lacked their genes. This background may have been responsible for a remark my adoptive mother made to me on several occasions when I was a child. She said, 'You know that if you had been our child, you would have been brilliant.' This probably was true, but the remark seemed very out of character, for she was very good to us. There

3

seemed to be an implicit assumption at that time that children who were put up for adoption would have inferior genetic inheritance. I had no comprehension of these matters as a child, but the general climate of thought, I am sure, did not help my self-esteem.

We used to visit a family of cousins who, in subtle ways, indicated that my siblings and I were inferior to them, and this was probably also due to the pervasive influence of eugenics at that time.

Partly through the experiences of growing up as an adopted child, I had little self-confidence, was rather shy and tended to feel somewhat apart, and was more an observer of what was going on than a participant. What I have written may give the impression that I had an unhappy childhood and that my adoptive parents were not good to me, but this was not so, because I had a happy childhood and rich and varied experiences. While growing up, for reasons I cannot now explain, I had a continuing worry that I was a financial drain on my adoptive parents. This, combined with my belief that I could not live up to my parents' expectations, influenced my decision to go to sea in the British Merchant Service, where I could become financially independent when I left school.

After leaving school, I served in the British Merchant Service from 1937 until 1946, initially as an apprentice and then as a third, second and first mate. In 1945, I married an American woman whom I had met in Vermont, while on leave after being torpedoed. She remained in the States while I returned to sea. We had agreed that whatever I did, it would be valuable for me to obtain a Master Mariner's certificate, so in 1946 I went ashore to study for the examinations. I passed the exams and then obtained a release from the Merchant Service, as the war was by now over. To obtain a shore job, it would be valuable to have a university degree, and my wife and I decided I should study for a degree in the USA. Harvard University accepted my application. The remaining problems of my getting to the States were finding a passage on a ship to the

States, and obtaining an immigration visa from the United States Consulate in Glasgow. The shipping company with whom I had worked, after a lot of persuasion, offered me a passage to New York on one of their ships, which was to sail in a week's time.

The only remaining obstacle was getting an immigration visa, and here the snag was the need to have proof of birthplace, because immigration quotas were based on where a person was born. Because I was an adopted child, I had an adoption certificate instead of a birth certificate. The former gave no information about place of birth, to help shield the identity of the birth parents. For weeks I had tried, through correspondence with the Registrar General's office, to obtain proof of my birthplace. This office maintains all records of births, deaths and marriages. They had refused my request, saying that it was illegal for them to divulge my birthplace. With the ship on which I was to sail leaving in a week, I decided to go to the headquarters of the Registrar General's office, which was still in Blackpool, where it had been relocated from London during the war. I little knew at the time that this visit would be the key to all that I learned years later, and is the topic of this book. For this reason, I will give the account of the visit by quoting from a letter I wrote to my wife on 2 April, 1946, on the way back from Blackpool. My wife kept my letters, and I found the letter only recently.

At 11:30 p.m. I caught the night train from Glasgow to Blackpool and after one change reached Blackpool at 5:00 a.m. this morning. The town was dead, and I walked the streets until I met a friendly policeman who directed me to a little all-night snack bar, where I drank tea, talked, and read... At 8:00 a.m., I was outside the hotel taken over by the Registrar General, and at 8:30 a.m., the civil servants started pouring in – first, the typists and clerks and last, the heads of departments. I explained my business to the door-keeper. He looked at the documents that I had brought and said he would introduce me to the man dealing with my case. When that man arrived, he curtly told me that I couldn't have the information unless I knew all the details, and even then a special court order must be given before the information could be divulged. In reply, I read him my rights and his duties from the Scottish Adoption Act. I had prepared myself for the visit by obtaining copies of the English and Scottish Adoption Acts. The Scottish law gave the right to every adopted person over the age of 17 to obtain their birth certificate, while in England, a special order of the court was needed, necessitating a lengthy and expensive procedure. He didn't say a word and hurried away. The doorkeeper, who had been listening, said, 'My, you've stirred something up now.' There was a great coming and going of officials hurrying by, and a few minutes later I was taken into an office and a senior official came in. I put my case very strongly, stressing the shortage of time, the delays they had caused, and the tremendous consequences of not getting proof of my birthplace – losing a place in college, missing my passage over, etc. The official asked to see the Adoption Act and I knew that my bluff was called. He saw it was the Scottish Act and not the English Act and explained the differences. I countered by pointing out that he had no right to mislead me in his previous correspondence, which had asked for details of my original parents and birthplace. If it was illegal to give me any of the information, why had he asked me for it. He knew some junior had made a mistake and conceded the error. Then I pushed home the injustice. He told me the lengthy procedure that I must go through with the Courts. I replied that if I had been told this by them when I first wrote to them over a month earlier, I could have done all this, but now there was no time and I must have the documentation now that the Scottish Consulate required. He pointed out the difficulty of searching for

6

the needed information with such scant evidence. The official, thinking me angry, tried to calm me down, so I immediately turned friendly, sympathized with his difficulties and understood how the mistakes had been made. Only I must have the certificate now. After nearly an hour's talk and others had been called in for consultation, they got to work on the phone and the search was on. Then followed nearly six hours of phoning and waiting. At last the answers came in, and the civil servant official was so pleased he forgot that he had infringed the law and ordered a copy to be mailed express to the Glasgow Consulate. He gave me a slip of paper on which he had written my birth name, 'Francis Sydney Wasley' and 'born in Skipton, Yorkshire'.

A few days later, I started on the voyage to New York, my wife, and my new home. The information I had received was consistent with the story that my adoptive aunt had given me when I had walked on the beach with her in the Isle of Wight.

2

I Start My Search at Skipton

From the time in 1946, when I learned of my original name and place of birth, until 1983, 37 years later, I gave little thought to the circumstances of my birth or my biological family. When I did think about it, I feared that were I to find my biological mother and make myself known to her, it might be hurtful to her. This concern lessened with time, because I felt that the older my biological mother grew, the less the news would hurt her. Also, I had no wish to hurt my adoptive parents as long as they were alive, in case they would interpret my search as an indication that I had not been content with their upbringing of me. By 1983, both of my adoptive parents were dead, and I guessed that my biological mother, if alive, would be in her eighties.

In the 1970s, my adoptive sister, Elaine, found a biological relative. This started her and her husband on a search for her biological family, and she succeeded in finding her mother, three sisters and several nieces and nephews. The search and the relationships she developed with her biological family opened up a whole new interest in her life. In correspondence and visits with Elaine it was apparent how much pleasure these experiences had given her, and I decided that I, too, should start a search for my family, armed with my adoptive aunt's story about my heritage and the piece of paper that gave the name given me by my birth mother and the place of my birth.

The first step in my search was to obtain a copy of my birth certificate from St Catherine's House in London, where the Office of Births, Deaths and Marriages was now located. I was able to do this because I had kept the piece of paper given me by the Registrar in 1946 when I went to see him at Blackpool. My excitement mounted as I opened the letter when it came with the certificate. This was the information that it contained:

'*When and Where Born*: Twenty-fourth of June, 1920, 11 Elliot Street, Skipton, Yorkshire. *Name*: Francis Sydney Wasley. *Sex*: Boy. *Name and Surname of Father*: [This was left a blank] *Name, Surname and Maiden Surname of Mother*: Teresa Gladys Wasley, Nurse Domestic. *Occupation of Father*: [This was left a blank] *Signature Description and Residence of Informant*: Teresa Gladys Wasley, 11 Elliot Street, Skipton. *When Registered*: Fifth of August, 1920.'

This information only corresponded in part with the story about my birth that my Aunt Hilda had told me when I was a child. Both sources agreed that I had been born in Yorkshire, but little else fitted together. My aunt had told me that my mother was the daughter of a titled Catholic family. If so, it seemed unlikely that she would give as her occupation 'Nurse Domestic'. My aunt had told me that my father was the family chauffeur, but this information was left blank. Perhaps the mother described by my aunt had tried to conceal my birth by persuading the nanny that she had employed to take me away and register herself as my mother. If this were the case, then the woman on the birth certificate would not be my mother. The blanks in place of my father's name and occupation might be a further way of concealing my birth. My birth had been registered 38 days after my date of birth, and this seemed a long time. It would have taken time for arrangements to be made for the family nanny to go somewhere where she could register the birth and enter her name as my mother.

In October 1983 I made a brief visit to Skipton. I knew very little about the town other that it was in Yorkshire, so I looked up some information. The town had a population of 13,210 in the early 1950s and lies in the midst of the Pennines, a spine of hills and mountains that runs north and south. It is at the southern end of the Yorkshire Dales, an area of great beauty and now a national park. Skipton, because it is the lowest way through the Pennines, has long been on an important trade route, and is a market town. During the time of canal building, one was built from Leeds to Liverpool, passing through Skipton and forming a link between the network of canals in the east and west. Wool and cotton have been a staple of local manufacture.

On the way to Skipton, I stopped at Wakefield, where the voting registers for towns in the West Riding of Yorkshire are kept. I wanted to see who had voted from the address of my birthplace, 11 Elliot Street. To my surprise, there was no Wasley who lived at that address. The only person listed was a Walter Mason. I then searched the register to see if there were any Wasleys who had voted in Skipton, and could find none for 1920, or for the next five years. There were, however, many Masons listed who had voted.

After leaving the office that kept the voting registers, I took the next train to Skipton, arrived after dark and found a nearby bed-and-breakfast lodging. The landlady was still up and showed me my room. I asked her where I could get something to eat, and she directed me to a nearby pub. The only space left to eat was a table, where a man I judged to be about 80 years old was sitting having a drink. He saw me looking for a place and kindly asked me to join him. He had always lived in Skipton, so I asked him if he had ever heard of anyone in the town by the name of Wasley. He thought for awhile and shook his head. By now it was getting late, and I was glad to get back to my lodging and off to bed.

The next morning I woke very early in order to go for a run. At that time I was training for a marathon and was running over 50 miles a week, and at Skipton I had the opportunity to get in some hill running. After running uphill for some time I looked down at the town, where I

10

could see the Liverpool and Leeds Canal, the churches standing out above the houses and the remains of a castle which was built in the 11th century. It was worth the trip just to be able to enjoy this beautiful view. I was glad that I had been born there. On my way back toward the town I saw ahead of me a tall, elderly man who was walking with long, easy strides and gave the impression of being an experienced walker. When I came up to him we exchanged greetings, and I felt that his was warm and friendly. When I got back to my night's lodging I changed quickly and went down for breakfast. The breakfast room was empty except for one middle-aged woman, so I asked if I might sit with her. She smiled and beckoned me to join her. Her name was Betty Birtwhistle, and during breakfast she told me that her great interest was genealogical research and that she had come to look up some family forebears. She lived near London and frequently went there to search various record sources. After she told me about her visit to Skipton, I told her the reasons for mine. She was most interested and offered to help me in any way she could. Before parting we exchanged addresses. I little knew then what a good friend she would become and how invaluable her help would be in my search.

I had to leave Skipton late that afternoon and had little time to waste, so decided to first find the house where I was born. Part of a terrace of small connected stone cottages, 11 Elliot Street was on a steep side street of the town. As I looked at the house I wondered why it had been chosen as the place of my birth? Who was this Walter Mason who lived at the cottage in 1920? Was Mason a trusted former employee of the titled Catholic family? I knocked on the door of number 11 and told the woman who answered that I was trying to get information about the family that had lived there in 1920. She said that she had only moved in recently, but her next-door neighbours had lived there a long time.

At this house I learned that a former resident was named Mrs Watson, and that her son worked in the local town

11

office. I thanked her, went to the office and found the man she had named. He told me where his mother lived and kindly checked the register of births and found the same information about my birth that I had obtained from the national office in London.

Before going to find his mother I decided to see if there was a record of my baptism at the local Roman Catholic church. This seemed likely from my aunt's story that my birth mother came from a Catholic family. The church was St Stephen's, a name that somehow seemed appropriate, and I approached it through an avenue of trees. The stone church was empty, but when I knocked at the door of the attached rectory, it was opened by Monsignor Murphy.

I explained why I had come, and he took me to the room where the register of baptisms was kept. He quickly found the record of my baptism on 1 August, 1920, four days before my birth had been registered. Beside my name of Francis Sydney Wasley there was recorded: 'Mother – Gladys Wasley (the name Teresa had been dropped); Godmother – Maria Mason.' There was no entry for godfather. It seemed reasonable that Maria Mason was the wife of Walter Mason of 11 Elliot Street.

The more I thought about the absence of Wasleys in Skipton, the more I realized I might have expected this. Whether or not Gladys Wasley was my mother, if she was trying to conceal my birth, she would go somewhere for my birth where there were no relatives. But why had she chosen to come to Walter Mason's home, and why had the person who was probably his wife acted as my godmother, and why had Walter not acted as my godfather?

To learn more about the Masons I went to the library and searched the current electoral register for Masons and Wasleys. There were several Masons listed, and I copied down their names and addresses. There were no Wasleys, and I noticed that whereas in the 1920 electoral register only men's names were listed, in the current register there were both men's and women's names. It was only later that I learned that the right to vote for all women was not

12

obtained in Britain until 1928. This explained why only Walter Mason was listed in the 1920 register. As a check on the list of Masons in the contemporary voting register, I looked at the listing under the same name in the telephone book.

I was anxious to contact anyone who might have been in Skipton and might have known about Gladys Wasley at the time of my birth. I found where Mrs Watson lived from the address her son had given me. She listened with interest while I told why I had come to visit her. She had lived on Elliot Street in 1920 and knew the Masons, but had no recollection of a visitor to the house who had a baby. She took me across the street to an old friend of hers who had also lived on Elliot Street, but she also had no memory of a woman visitor to the Masons who had a baby. She suggested the name of someone else who knew Elliot Street in 1920, and when I found her she also gave the same response to my question. I was passed on in this way until I had talked to five elderly ladies, but none of them had any memory of my mother.

By this time I was hungry and needed time to think how I might best spend the few hours remaining before my train left. On the way back to the centre of town I crossed a stone bridge over the canal, where a number of brightly painted canal barges were tied up to the towpath. A family carrying provisions for the next stage of their voyage was returning to one of the barges, with a small and excited dog running in circles around them. Along the towpath, the crew of a barge were mopping down the deck. I turned onto the high street, which was wide and lined with stone houses and shops, with white, painted façades a hotel and eating places. A war memorial was prominent in the middle of the street, and a stone church marked the upper end of the street. I found the same pub where I had eaten before. I kept wondering about whether or not Gladys Wasley was my mother and whether baptismal records were sometimes falsified. This question took me back to St Stephen's Church. The Monsignor was out, so I asked the

13

priest who was there whether falsification of information would be regarded as a grave sin for a Catholic. He replied that various arrangements were sometimes made.

I was having no luck finding anyone who might have some information about Gladys Wasley, so decided to see what I might learn from the many Masons in town. In the telephone book there were 12 local listings, and I copied the information. There were also other regional telephone books. If Gladys Wasley had chosen to come to Skipton because there were no relatives in the area, then it would be reasonable to presume that there would also be an absence of Wasleys in a wide area around Skipton. The phone books of Bradford, Blackburn, Manchester, Leeds and Harrogate collectively only listed ten Wasleys, so this supported my hunch.

Turning back to the list of Masons, it was difficult to know where to start. To get some advice, I decided to go to the local police station. I explained to the sergeant on duty why I had come, and after conferring with some colleagues he told me that the best person to see was John Mason, who ran a printing business with his son. John was in his seventies, had lived all his life in Skipton, and knew a great many people. They phoned to see if he was at his printing business, which he was. I thanked the police and followed their directions to John Mason's business address, where the door was opened by a man who took me to John Mason's office. To our mutual surprise, we realized that we had already met. He was the man that I had passed early that morning when I was running up in the hills. I explained why I had been running that morning, and he told me that every working day he walked to and from home, a distance of six miles. He loves walking and goes all over the Dales, sometimes accompanied by his grandchildren. He lives in an old farmhouse up on the hills above Skipton with his son, daughter-in-law, and two grandchildren. His wife died three years ago. He has handed over his printing business to his son John, but still comes in to work.

He asked me if there was anything he could do for me. I told him why I had come to Skipton, and as I told him he became intensely interested and told me what he could remember. In 1920, he was seven years old and a frequent visitor to 11 Elliot Street, to see his uncle Walter and Aunt Mae. He had no recollection of seeing a young woman visitor or a baby at the house. He phoned his sister, who had always lived in Skipton, repeated the story that I had told him, and asked her if she had any memory of a birth taking place at the Masons' in June of 1920. She did not, and had no idea of who Gladys Wasley might be. She suggested that I go and see Florence Steele, who had lived at 9 Elliot Street in 1920.

John kindly drove me to where she now lived in Skipton, and told her why we had come. She remembered Walter and Mary Mason very well and often saw them at that time, but she could not remember any woman giving birth there, or seeing a baby. They remembered that Walter was a farmer who went away as a soldier during World War One. While away he met and married Mary, whom he brought back to Skipton after the war. They rented 11 Elliot Street. The terrace houses were back-to-back and had a small living room and kitchen downstairs, two bedrooms upstairs and a small attic. There was no indoor bathroom or plumbing. Later, after the Masons had left, the local council bought the terrace houses and expanded each house so that each was the full, rather than half the width of the building, and installed plumbing. When the Masons came to their house they only had a bed. To make a sideboard they put three orange crates together and covered them. Walter returned to his work as a farmer. They remembered Mae (as they called her) as a very kind-hearted person who was rather heavy. Mae was a Catholic, but not Walter. The Masons had five children, but the oldest child probably was born after June 1920.

I asked whether any of the family was still in Skipton. They replied that later on Walter and Mae had separated, and they thought that Mae had gone to Bristol. By this time, I had to get to the station if I was to catch the train, so I thanked John Mason and Florence Steele for all their help, and made my way to the station. During the train journey, I wrote an account of the day and mulled over what I had learned. It was puzzling why none of the people that I had contacted had any memories of Gladys Wasley, or my birth, especially when it appeared that Gladys had stayed with the Masons for over a month. I pondered the next moves that I should take in the search, and soon fell asleep with the rhythmic sound of the train. A few days later I returned to my home in the USA.

I wrote to Betty Birtwhistle, giving her an account of my visit. She was curious about Walter Mason's wife, Mary, and found the entry at the Register of Births, Deaths and Marriages. She obtained a copy of the marriage certificate and sent it to me.

Mary Mason gave as her father's name, Frank Wasley, artist. So Mary Mason was my mother's sister, and this explained why my mother had gone to her at the time of my birth, and why Mary was my godmother.

3

Who Was My Mother?

I needed to find out more about Gladys Wasley, named as my mother on my birth certificate, and wondered how to go about it. My wife suggested that since her father's occupation was given as artist, we might find some reference to him in an art book. She went to our local library and found *Dictionaire des Peinteures, Sculptures Dessenateurs* that listed the names and prices of works of the artists. Frank Wasley was included in the listing as 'British, born 1850, died 1934'. Fifteen paintings were listed as sold, with the titles, including land and seascapes.

In my next letter to Betty Birtwhistle, I passed on my wife's suggestion about learning more about Frank Wasley, and her next letters dramatically advanced my search. Betty went to her local library, where two very helpful assistants took a lot of trouble searching reference books and uncovered little new information. But one of the assistants knew of an art gallery in Reigate where the dealer had told him about Frank Wasley's work. Betty went to visit him, and he was most helpful giving her the name of a lady who is apparently something of an expert on Wasley's paintings. Her name was Rosalind Jordan. Betty got in touch with her and learned, to her delight, that Jordan was in touch with a daughter of Frank Wasley. Betty wrote, 'I have, therefore, written to her, asking if she would be kind enough to put me in touch, explaining the circumstances and stressing that you are anxious to discover details of Gladys Wasley, who is possibly your mother. It may be a while before I have a reply as, no doubt, she will wish to contact them for their permission to put us in touch, but I am hopeful of a satisfactory outcome. What a strange chance it was, to find that library assistant! I am sure there is an element of fate in your endeavours – witness the meeting of your Mason cousin that day in Skipton.'

The Wasley that Betty had found was a younger sister of Gladys, a Winifred Folks. Prior to my meeting Winifred, she wrote to me and enclosed a photograph of Gladys (see Fig 1). I was entirely unprepared for the strength of the emotional response that swept through me when I looked at the photo. I felt a deep certainty that Gladys was my mother, and was the person that I had always pictured in my imagination. The photo was taken when she was a young woman, and she looked kindly, calm and, I thought, very beautiful. Others beside myself saw a resemblance between Gladys and myself. I still somewhat distrusted my intuitive sense that Gladys was my mother until the following incident:

An adoptive niece who knew my children well was shown the photo of Gladys, and without being told anything about the picture, was asked, 'Do you know who this is?' Without any hesitation she replied, 'Beth – but why is she wearing that dress?' Beth is my younger daughter. Later, when I obtained other photos of Gladys, some showed a remarkable likeness to my younger son and to myself.

I now knew that my adoptive Aunt Hilda had got the identity of my mother wrong. Yet I was still loath to abandon everything in her story, because I believed my aunt had reported truthfully what she believed to be the facts of my parentage. I tried to think of ways in which what I now knew could be fitted into my aunt's story, and an intriguing possibility occurred to me. My mother as a nurse domestic could have worked for the titled Catholic family in Yorkshire. Her photograph showed that she was a beautiful woman who would have been attractive to men. My father might have been someone in the family who employed her.

Shortly after this, John Mason of Skipton wrote me the

18

following: 'It is interesting to note the association of a very prominent Catholic family with your mother. Presumably, the Catholic house referred to is called Broughton Hall, surrounded by a considerable estate. The family name is Tempest (we do their printing). The estate is situated only a few miles outside Skipton.' Possibly my mother had heard about the job at Broughton Hall through her sister.

In his letter, John Mason invited me to visit him on my next trip to England, and I took advantage of his kind offer. When I arrived at Skipton, I told John that I would like to meet the Tempest family.

By good fortune, his son, John Junior, who had taken over the family business, had just completed a printing order for the Tempests and was planning to deliver the order that morning. He phoned Henry Tempest and, introducing me as his cousin, said that I wanted to find out whether my mother had worked at Broughton Hall around 1919. He replied that he was terribly busy but that he would see me if we came over right away. We drove over to Broughton Hall, only a few miles outside Skipton, and turned in through the main gate. The Hall was at the lower part of a sloping hillside, with great trees on the hill behind the house and large lawns stretching out in front. We followed a long curving driveway that led to the main entrance, which was covered by a two-storey portico supported by large stone pillars. The house was built of stone and had been added onto at different times. The main house had three storeys and chimney pots bristled from the roofs. This part of the house dated from the 16th century. There were extensions at each end, and at one end there was an attached chapel with a tower that was higher than any other part of the house. The house was part of a 3000-acre estate, which included a residence for the family Catholic priest, large gardens, trout fishing and an old English pub set in the Yorkshire Dales. It was truly a stately home. It reminded me of Castle Howard which was used as the setting for many of the episodes of the BBC dramatization of *Brideshead Revisited*.

John stopped the van at the front door, and we climbed the steps to the large stone entrance. The portico made me feel very small, and I wondered whether that had been one of the reasons why it had been designed that way. I expected a large metal handle that would set a large bell clanging in the house. Instead, there was a very ordinary electric bell that we rang. Henry Tempest, to whom we had spoken on the phone, answered the door and explained why he was so busy: the kitchen was being converted to the way it looked at the beginning of the century, and was being used in the filming of a production. There were painters in the house, and he was remodelling the wing near the chapel for rental purposes.

I again explained that I thought that my mother might have been in domestic service at the house in 1919, and he considered how he might be able to find out. While he was doing this I looked at Henry's appearance with considerable interest, because of the outside possibility that he might be a half-brother. We did have similarities in appearance. Henry felt the best place to look for records of my mother would be in the family archives that were kept on the third floor in a room that had been servants' quarters. We entered the room, and Henry told me that that was where my mother might have slept. The archives included diaries of his parents and forebears, and the account books of the estate.

He found the gardener's accounts that covered the years 1919 and 1920, but not the housekeeper's accounts, where my mother's wages would have been recorded. Henry had no further time to search, so we returned downstairs. Opposite the front door was a huge glass conservatory. Henry expressed concern about the safety of the family archives and the need for microfilming in case of fire. I suggested that he might get the advice of an archivist. He also told me of the financial problems he encountered when he inherited the estate and was faced with raising money to pay for the 60 per cent death taxes. Running the estate sounded such a headache I began to fear that if he learned

20

that I had a family connection, he might be delighted to hand over the headache to me. Later I learned from a lawyer that if an illegitimate child is legally adopted, he or she forfeits all inheritance rights from the biological parents, so I was safe. After thanking Henry we took our leave and drove back to Skipton. On the way John Junior remembered that Stephen Tempest, who my mother may have cared for, used to drive to and fro from Skipton in a white Rolls-Royce. He always drove in the middle of the road and never exceeded 35 mph, so he was well remembered by other users of that road.

After they drove me back to Skipton I had a few hours left before my train left.

I decided to look through the 1919 and 1920 copies of the local newspaper, the *Craven Chronicle*, to see if I might learn more about the Tempest family at the time my mother might have been with them. I was unsuccessful, but scanning the copies of the paper gave me some sense of those times. The content included accounts of efforts to help stranded prisoners of war, notices of deaths of soldiers reported missing during the war, the shortage of housing, the raising of money for a war memorial and its unveiling, prize-giving at schools, court hearings on abuse or neglect of children, local musical and theatrical performances, sports and obituaries. I thanked the manager of the paper for letting me see the old copies, and left.

With the time remaining, I went to the Catholic church and asked the priest whether there were any lists of parishioners in 1919–20. This was a long shot, because my mother would probably have attended the family chapel at Broughton Hall. Again, I had no luck. Walking back to the station, I felt depressed, feeling that I had made so little progress in my search. When I reached the station I found John Mason Junior waiting for me. He told me that Henry Tempest's wife had called at their print shop that afternoon. She thanked them for the print order that we had delivered, and said that Henry had told her about me, and that she would try and find out about my mother. She

21

would phone her aunt, who was 90 years old and used to travel to and fro from London with Roger Stephen Tempest and his family. She would remember their nanny at that time. She also said that if I returned with my wife, or alone, she hoped that we would have tea with them at Broughton Hall.

During the train ride, I realized, belatedly, that if my mother had worked for the Tempest family, she would have visited her sister in Skipton and would have been remembered by some in the Mason family. Later, I corresponded with the Tempest's aunt and sent her a photo of my mother. We talked on the phone, and she said that she was sure that my mother had not been a nanny to the family because my mother had such a striking face that she would never have forgotten her.

Later, I found out who my mother did work for prior to her pregnancy, and it was in the Thames Valley, not in Yorkshire. I put my adopted aunt's story about the titled Catholic family to rest. It was only far later in my search that I found a possible explanation for the source of my aunt's story.

4

Finding My Mother's Sister, Winifred

To learn more about my biological family, I decided first to focus my search on my mother, Gladys Wasley, a nurse domestic whose father was an artist. By finding and contacting Rosamund Jordan, the art dealer, Betty opened up the next phase of my search. In a letter to me, Betty wrote, 'This morning I have had a response to my letter to the art dealer, who lives at Stockton on Tees, enclosing these photos of Frank Wasley's pictures and telling me that you have two aunts still living here in England. One is Lena, and the other, whose address I enclose, is named Winifred Folks. I am today writing to her, and am told that she is very excited at the news of a nephew in America. I am hoping that she will be able to put us in touch with Lena. I feel almost as excited as you must be, and am astonished at the chances that led us to the discovery of your relatives. I am so glad for you and hope that you will, at last, be able to learn about your mother's story.'

She then gave me the address of Winifred, who lived on the south coast at Hove, near Brighton.

A week later, another letter arrived from Betty with the news that she had heard from Winifred Folks. 'She is delighted to know of your existence and is eagerly looking forward to hearing from you. There are a number of things she has to show you if you come over some time.'

A few days later, another letter arrived from Betty. She told me that Winifred Folks had written to say that Frank Wasley had married twice. The first marriage was

23

just before he went on a visit to Canada. There were two children from this marriage – a boy who died and Edith, who was sent to a convent in Northampton when they returned from Canada. (Later, I was unable to find any evidence that there was a son.) His second wife was the mother of four girls – Mary, Gladys, Winifred and Lena. In hopes of finding my mother's family, Betty had phoned a number of Wasleys she found in the phone book; she had received an unexpected response from a man who had been interested in the genealogy of the Wasley family. He told Betty of the two marriages of Frank Wasley, but was puzzled because his first wife appeared to have lived for years after Frank's second marriage. Betty commented that 'there seems to be so much mystery surrounding the family that one hardly knows truth from fiction. ... I do hope that you are able to untangle this rather bewildering web of facts and eventually discover your real parentage'.

I had written to Winifred Folks as soon as Betty had sent me her address and her permission to write. With the letter, I had sent a photograph of myself taken when I was in my thirties. Every day I eagerly looked for a letter from Winifred, and it came soon after Betty's letter. She wrote,

Dear Stephen,

All this was a surprise to Lena and me (but a very pleasant one). We knew very little of our big sisters, they were always together – they went to boarding school. I travelled round England with my parents, living in furnished houses for a six-month tenantry. Lena was born at this time. Finally we settled down at Henley on Thames, where my parents died.

So glad to get your photograph, very good looking and like your mother. Same well-shaped oval head; the lower part of the face is exactly like hers. She had blue eyes, light brown hair and good colouring. She was about 5'6" in height. She was very sweet and gentle – how proud she would have been of you.

I hope to be able to show you some interesting snapshots of our family. Your grandmother was your grandfather's second wife, Irish, her father was in the army. I found a cutting of a description of his military funeral in Bristol. The coffin was placed on a gun carriage with his sword on the Union Jack. It was drawn by the Marines to the cemetery. He was in the Crimean War – this goes back a long way. Your grandfather was very talented – his first love was music, only in his forties did he turn to painting at which he made his name. He was a keen fisherman, in Yorkshire our larder was always stocked with salmon and trout. From him you undoubtedly inherited his love of music.

I am 86 and tire very easily. Hence, this badly written letter! A stroke I had 2 years ago made me slow down quite a lot, but with the help and encouragement of my friends I have gained confidence. I have just given up my car, how I miss it. I play bridge, only friendly, but life is very pleasant.

How kind of Betty Birtwhistle to help you with your research to find your mother – Lena and I don't want any more – we feel we are so disinterested in our relatives that we would rather leave things as they are.

I look forward to meeting you very much – there will be many snapshots I can show you of your mother and the rest of your family – so let me know when you are likely to be in England.

With affection from your new-found aunt,

Winifred.

I was so excited to receive this letter and felt that I had reached a milestone in my search. It was wonderful to know that I was welcome and would have the opportunity to meet my aunt. The one thing that puzzled me about the letter was the reference to not wanting me to do any more research, and this feeling being also that of her younger sister Lena. What was it that they did not want me to find out? Maybe I would find out when I met my aunt.

I hastened to reply to my aunt's letter as follows:

Dear Aunt Winifred,

Thank you so much for your warm, affectionate letter. It is wonderful of you to give me such a welcome after all these years. When I saw the photograph of my mother I was startled by the power of the emotion that swept through me. I had some deep inner feeling that I knew her. As a child I always imagined what my real mother was like. Someone who was kind, loving and beautiful, and yesterday my mother looking at me, as captured by the camera, was the person I had imagined. My wife and several friends to whom I have shown the photograph of my mother felt that there was a striking resemblance to me and how like she is to my younger daughter, Beth. I enclose a photo of Beth taken last summer. I am at the head of the table. Since then I have removed my beard.

It was lovely of you to tell me about my mother, yourself and the family, and I look forward to meeting you and Aunt Lena. There is a good chance that I will be able to visit you sometime in the next few weeks. I will write again when I have a firm date. I don't want to overtire you, so possibly it would be more convenient if I made several brief visits over more than one day. I have friends in Brighton with whom I will stay. I do hope that I will be able to meet Aunt Lena.

I sincerely hope that my finding you does not cause you any distress or embarrassment. It was because I did not want to give any hurt to my mother that I have waited so many years before starting my search. I would be very upset if I were to hurt you in any way, and I deeply appreciate your generosity in letting me write and come and see you. It will be very exciting for me to see the snapshots you refer to.

So looking forward to our meeting,

Affectionately, Stephen.

On the same day, I wrote to Betty Birtwhistle to give her the news.

5

Visits with Aunt Winifred

Less than a month after writing to Aunt Winifred, I was able to visit her at her home in Hove. Her flat was one of many in a building that overlooked the sea. Aunt Winifred greeted me warmly and led me down a passage to her living room. She was a tall, imposing, handsome woman with white hair and clearly rather frail, and she quickly made me feel at ease.

I told my aunt that I was eager to learn all I could about my mother. In preparation for my visit, my aunt had gone through some of her photograph albums to find pictures that would be of interest to me. She said that she hoped that I would not be disappointed, but she had never known my mother well. She reminisced about her family and showed me some of the photographs from her albums. One was of the man my mother married. The two most important pieces of information I gained were that the man my mother married was not my father, because she first met him three years after I was born. From their marriage they had a daughter, Margaret, so I had a half-sister. The rest of her family news and what I learned from the photographs I will give in later chapters.

Aunt Lena, the youngest, was, Aunt Winifred told me, a recluse and did not wish to see me. She is a widow and has two children. Her son teaches English in Oman; her daughter is married to a doctor and lives near Newcastle.

I did not want to tire my aunt unduly, so did not stay very long. As I was leaving, she showed me an oil painting of Venice which had been painted by her father. It had a slight tear in the canvas, so she felt that it would be of no value to anyone except herself.

After leaving my aunt, I had very mixed feelings. I was touched by the warmth and affection that she had shown to a nephew who had been totally unknown to her until a few weeks previously. I was excited that at last I had met a member of my biological family and that I was getting some glimpse of my mother and her family from what I had just heard and the photos I had seen. On the other hand, I was disappointed by how little I had learned about my mother and how out of touch my aunt was with all her family except Aunt Lena, whom I had hoped to meet, only to be told that she did not wish to see me. I was also sorry that my aunt had lost touch with my half-sister, whom I was eager to meet if she was still alive. However, I hoped to have further visits with my aunt, and there would be other things that she would be able to tell me.

I had kept in close contact by mail with Betty Birtwhistle about the progress in my search, and she kindly went to the Register of Births, Deaths and Marriages, which after World War Two relocated in London. These findings confirmed and gave specific dates for some of what Aunt Winifred had told me. My mother was born in 1893. Her father, Frank Stephen Wasley, was an artist and married to Sarah, née Campion. My mother married Bernard Mahon when she was 33, and they had a child, Margaret Patricia. My mother died of cancer in 1933, aged 39. Betty Birtwhistle, in the accompanying letter, wrote:

> I am sorry to be the bearer of the news of your mother's death so long ago and thus dashing the hopes of a possible meeting, but she would have been ninety by now and might not have withstood the encounter if she were frail or in poor health. . . . Hoping to hear from you before long and with every good wish.
> Yours most affectionately,
> Betty Birtwhistle.

I was saddened that my mother had died, because I would have liked to have met her and thanked her for giving me life.

Six months later I was in England with my wife, and we were staying with friends near Hove, where Aunt Winifred lived. I was eager to see her again and to introduce my wife to her. I phoned her several times to arrange a visit, but each time the phone seemed out of order. On the day we had to leave the vicinity we decided to make a call on Winifred without advance notice. When we arrived at her flat we rang the bell and then heard Winifred's voice on a speaker arrangement near the bell. She asked who we were, and I answered. To our sorrow and surprise she said that she did not want to see us, and told us to go away. Her voice sounded very upset and agitated. After the warm welcome she had given me on my first visit, this rejection was totally unexpected and shocking, and we left.

At that time there seemed no explanation to my aunt's behaviour, and it was only later, when I met Lena's son and daughter, that they suggested why my aunt had turned us away. Several years later, Aunt Lena told me that she had been with her sister when this incident occurred and she had been very upset by her sister's behaviour. At the time we called, Winifred was in the midst of her weekly bridge game with her regular players. These were Russian aristocrats who had fled to England after the Revolution, and some still retained their titles. Our visit would not only have interrupted the bridge game, but might have resulted in her guests learning that Winifred had a bastard nephew. Winifred held the conventions of morality of her day.

Lena being there may have also contributed to Winifred's behaviour. In her first letter to me she had written that Lena was a recluse and did not wish to see me, and this was probably her way of discouraging me from going any further in my search. If I had met Lena at the flat I would soon have realized that Lena was not as Winifred had depicted her, and that the meeting would likely have led to further meetings with Lena. This Winifred did not want.

Lena's daughter later gave other more salient reasons, which we will come to later. When I returned home, I wrote to Winifred, telling her how sorry I was that I had distressed her by our visit. A few months later I learned the sad news that she had died.

6

Finding Aunt Lena

From what I had learned, it was clear that the person who would know most about my mother would be her older sister, Mary, or Mae as she was called by the family. But I did not know whether she was alive or how I could find her, because I did not know what surname she assumed if she had had a second marriage. The only person who would have any information about my Aunt Mae was the youngest of my aunts, Lena, so I set about trying to find her, knowing she was still alive.

Aunt Winifred had told me that Lena was a recluse and did not wish to see me. I did not know where she lived or her married name. My only hope of learning more about her was if Winifred had left some information about her in her will. Some time after Aunt Winifred died, I went to Somerset House in London, where all wills are available to the public. I was told there that to obtain a will, the first step was to find the number of the will. These are listed in large ledgers arranged chronologically, which are in shelves at the back of long lines of desks. In each ledger, the deaths are listed alphabetically. Beside each entry is a reference number.

When I found the entry for Aunt Winifred, I filled in the information from the register entry onto a form and took it to a desk. The civil servant who received me first sent me down a corridor to a window, where I paid the fee required for obtaining a copy of a will and was given a receipt. I took this back to the desk, where they took my application form and told me they would call out my name when they had the will. I expected a long wait, but in a surprisingly short time my name was called, and they handed me a copy of Winifred's will. I had previously looked for wills of my mother, my grandfather and his wife, and in each case found that they had left no will, more technically known as having died intestate. Winifred had left half of her estate to her sister, Lena, and the will gave her address. The remaining half she divided equally between Lena's two children, Joanna and Jonathan, and the will gave their addresses.

There was a chance that Joanna might be sympathetic toward my desire to learn about my mother, and that she might persuade her mother to let me see her. I could think of no better way of getting to see Aunt Lena, so I wrote to Joanna. The letter began by saying that I had recently learned that we were related and that I was writing to ask her to help me learn more about my mother. I then briefly sketched my life history, including the search for my biological family, and briefly what I had found. I described my meeting with Aunt Winifred and part of her letter that led to the meeting. I then continued:

> I would very much like to meet you, to share with you what I have learned about the Wasley family and learn anything from you that you can tell me about my mother and the Wasleys. I would also be grateful to you for any advice you can give me about whether your mother might be willing to share with me what she knows about Margaret, my half-sister, and our mother. If your mother is unwilling to see me would she give you the information and you, in turn, give it to me? Naturally I am interested in learning who my father was and whether there might be any clues that Aunt Lena might be able to provide. In any case, it would mean a lot to me if I could meet you.

Enclosed in the letter was a photo of my mother. In case Joanna had misgivings about the genuineness of the content of the letter, I included the names, addresses and phone numbers of my adoptive sister and a distinguished professional colleague.

In Joanna's reply she wrote that she understood my desire to find out more about the Wasley family and my mother in particular. Unfortunately, she really had nothing to tell me. She was only two or three when my mother died, and during the past 20 years she had seen very little of Aunt Winifred. Aunt Mae and my mother were never talked about except in passing. She said that Aunt Mae was ostracized for some reason ('I gather she was thought to have married beneath her – a sin in those days.') Joanna's mother had contacted Aunt Mae after her first husband had died, and she had married again. Joanna had never met any of Aunt Mae's children. She wrote that she was going to visit her mother and would see what she could learn from her that might be of help to me.

Some time later I heard again from Joanna. She kindly invited me to visit her and her husband, and wrote that her mother would like to meet me. It seemed wise to visit Joanna before Aunt Lena, and on my next trip to England I visited Joanna's home, travelling by train to the nearest large town and from there on using a hired car.

The large stone house was comfortably situated beside the village green and behind a tall hedge. Joanna, or Jo as she preferred to be called, met me at the door (see Fig 2). She was tall, with wavy grey hair and strong facial features. She wore slacks and a sweater, and the similarity in our appearances was apparent. She welcomed me warmly, and the welcome was added to by a young and excited golden retriever. Jo took me into the large kitchen where she gave me some soup and a light cold meal, which was very welcome after travelling since early morning. She made me feel very much at home and was easy to get along with.

After I had eaten, we moved into the comfortable living room, where we were soon joined by Jo's husband, Gilbert. They had moved to the village of Dunstan after Gilbert's retirement. Golf clubs and a fishing rod stood in the hall,

34

and I learned that they were ardent golfers, using a nearby course that would be termed a links because of its proximity to the sea and the setting among sand dunes – very much like the traditional Scottish golf course. They had five children, two of whom had emigrated to New Zealand. Among the pictures in the living room were several by our grandfather, Frank Wasley. One was of people sitting on a beach looking out to sea, another was of fishing boats at sea, and a third was of a rough sea. I had brought with me the photos that I had collected of the Wasleys, which I showed them, and they corroborated and added to what Aunt Winifred had told.

I asked Jo why she thought that my wife and I had been turned away on my second visit to Aunt Winifred and why her voice had sounded so frightened. Jo said that as Winifred aged she became increasingly paranoid about her possessions, and before anyone visited she would lock up anything of value. This was later confirmed by her brother, Jonathan, who added that Winifred suffered from migraine headaches. When suffering with them she would still play bridge, but would be under severe stress. Jo gave me her mother's address and phone number, and said that she would tell her mother about my visit.

After returning home, I wrote to Joanna and Gilbert to thank them for their hospitality. Several months later I wrote again, with additional information I had obtained about the Wasley family and plans for my next visit to England. I ended by hoping that Jo's mother would be willing to see me. No answer came to my letter, and I became concerned as the date of my departure neared. Just before leaving, a letter from Jo arrived. She invited me to visit them again and stay overnight, and wrote that she had phoned her mother, who said that she would like to meet me. Jo gave her mother's address and phone number in Buckinghamshire, and wrote that her brother, Jonathan, was now living with her mother, so that there was a good chance that I could meet him as well. There was no time to write back, so when I arrived in England I phoned and made arrangements to first visit Jo and her husband and then go on and meet Aunt Lena.

After an overnight stay with Jo and Gilbert, I continued south by train to London, where I phoned Aunt Lena. Jonathan answered the call. We settled on a date and time, and he gave me instructions about using the London Underground service to the place nearest where they lived, and where he would meet me with his car. We had no difficulty in recognizing each other (see Fig 3), and we were soon in the countryside passing large fields and a village, where a windmill stood at the highest point. The only part that I saw of the village where they lived was a single street with widely spaced houses. Aunt Lena's house was separated from the road by a white picket fence. It was built of brick with windows that had small diamond-shaped panes and chimneys that stretched up above the house. We entered a driveway beside the house, and Jonathan stopped the car in front of a small wooden garage. Aunt Lena came out of the back door into the garden to welcome me. She was of average height, shorter than her elder sister, Winifred, and her daughter, Jo. She had a strong, alert face with hazel, enquiring eyes and greying, wavy hair brushed back. She did not look her 82 years. In a letter to me, she described her daily life as follows:

> Jonathan and I work most of the time here on household and garden chores. He has a lot of asthma to cope with and I cannot walk very far. I manage with the help of a stick to shop in Winslow. I can garden when the weather permits and do our cooking.

Jonathan told me that his mother was rather deaf, but this did not seem to get in the way of our conversing.

As soon as I entered the house I felt the presence of my grandfather, Frank. He was looking down at us from a self-portrait. It was done in charcoal when I guessed him to be in his sixties. He seemed calm and grave, and the portrait was very much alive. Aunt Lena had lunch all ready in the dining room, and after we had eaten, we moved into the living room for coffee and an afternoon of talk. They knew of my eagerness to learn more about my mother, and Aunt Lena did her best to remember all that she could. She was at a disadvantage because she was trying to recall memories of persons, places and events that had occurred over half a century ago. Also, being eleven years younger than my mother, her earliest memories of my mother would be when Lena was about 10 years old and my mother about 21. Each memory that my aunt recalled seemed to trigger off another. Bits and pieces of her history and that of her family's history emerged in no particular sequence.

At first I would ask questions to try and clarify or expand something that she said, but I soon realized that this impeded the flow of her thought and that she was unable to answer my questions. Jonathan sat with us and said very little, and when he did it was to help his mother remember some date or incident. Lena did not take herself as seriously as Aunt Winifred, had a nice sense of humour, and was able to laugh at herself and her family. She did not seem to be a recluse, but rather someone who enjoyed company and was outgoing and friendly. I wondered whether Aunt Winifred's characterization of her sister had been to discourage me from trying to get in touch with her.

After my first visit I left with a feeling of affection for my aunt, and I also found it very easy to get along with her son Jonathan, who kindly drove me back to the station. I had four subsequent visits to my aunt and Jonathan, and my affection steadily grew. On some of the visits I stayed overnight, and on one my wife came with me, and also felt Lena's warmth, humour and kindness and greatly liked Jonathan. Lena was generous in sharing with me her memories of my mother, her family and her own life. She showed me the sketchbooks of her father, and I learned that some of the pictures on the walls had been painted by her and that she had inherited some of her father's talent.

37

On one of my visits, Lena said that she had something of my mother's that she wished me to have. She then handed me a brooch that I immediately recognized. In the first photograph that I had seen of my mother she was wearing that brooch on her dress. It was gold with a citrine stone in the middle. It was a deeply emotional moment for me to be given something that had clearly meant so much to my mother, and by the wonderful kindness and generosity of my aunt. She then said that she had something else that she wanted to give me, and unwrapped a silver tea service which had been given to her when she was married. I was touched that she should do this for a nephew she had never known and only met recently for a few visits. I took the presents home and gave the brooch to my half-sister, asking her eventually to leave it to my one granddaughter, who would also receive the tea set from me. I felt that my mother would have liked this.

The more that Lena shared with me what she knew about the family, the more we were able to evaluate and discuss the information that we now shared. In the other searches that I was making I would bring what I found to Lena by letter or during a visit, and Lena, Jonathan and I would review and try to interpret these findings. This in turn would often spark additional memories from my aunt. In all, I learned more about my mother and her family from Lena than from anyone else. For me, each visit was like an exciting voyage of exploration, and I had some fear that I was exploiting my aunt. I shared this concern with Jonathan, but he pointed out that for his mother it was a rare and rewarding experience to be with a person who was obviously very fond of her, had a tremendous interest in her history and was happy to listen intently hour after hour to her talking.

I first met Aunt Lena in 1987, when she was 83 years old. When she died in 1996, I grieved deeply for someone that I had come to love and cherish.

7

Finding My Half-sister, Margaret

I had been excited to learn that my mother had had a second child, Margaret, so I had a half-sister. This was reason enough for wanting to find her. If she could share memories of our mother with me, so much the better. I realized that Margaret was only seven years old when our mother died, so she would be limited in the period she would have known our mother.

Neither of my aunts knew anything about Margaret's life after her childhood. Betty Birtwhistle searched the records at the Register, but could find no record of her death. By this time, Betty was suffering increasingly from arthritis of the hip and became unable to travel, so her enquiries took the form of writing letters and phoning. She understood that the Salvation Army had a good record of being able to trace long-lost relatives. She wrote to them explaining the circumstances, but they replied saying that they were very sorry not to be able to help because they never took on a commitment where there might be too great a shock for someone – in this case my half-sister.

Betty had read an article in *The Times* about a woman who had traced her mother through the Catholic Children's Society Crusade of Rescue. She learned that they had access to the old London County Council records, which contained records of children who had been given treatment, were hospitalized or were in similar institutions. Betty recalled that in one of my letters I mentioned that Aunt Winifred had told me that after the death of Margaret's mother she was very disturbed and might have had

39

some kind of treatment. As a long shot, Betty wrote to them, explaining why she was making the search for me. They replied that they had no information about Margaret in their files.

We were having little luck in our search, but were realistic enough to know that the odds were against our finding Margaret and that we would need to be patient and follow up every possible lead. It was possible that the convent school that Margaret attended in Littlehampton after her mother's death might give us some clues to her whereabouts, so Betty looked in the Yellow Pages telephone book and found the phone number of the Sisters of the Holy Family in Littlehampton. She called them and found that they had been there since 1904. The Sister who answered listened to Betty's story and offered to search their early records. Some time later Betty received a written reply. They had drawn a blank in their search. They had got in touch with an elderly Sister who was at the convent school at the time that Margaret would have been there, and although she had a very good memory, she had no recollection of Margaret.

On a visit to London, I went to St Catherine's House and found a record of marriage for Margaret Patricia Mahon. It gave an address for her, and if I had identified the right person it should be easy to find her. The registers containing the records at St Catherine's House only give limited information, and to obtain all the information it is necessary to order and pay for a full copy of the marriage certificate. It was several weeks before this arrived, and at first glance I could see that the Margaret on the copy of the entry of marriage was not my half-sister. The date of her birth and her father's occupation did not fit what I knew about her. This was a great disappointment.

I cannot remember where I learned that a special section of the British Department of Health and Social Security, located in Newcastle, would forward a letter to anyone in Britain who had a Social Security number. It would then be up to the person who received the letter to decide whether they would answer or not. I wrote to them, explaining why I was trying to find my half-sister, and enclosed a sealed letter to her, explaining who I was and hoping that she would be willing to meet me. Several months later they sent me a form letter saying that 'We have no record of this person's present address. The letter you sent for forwarding is returned herewith.'

I wrote and told Betty and shared my disappointment with her. She replied, pointing out that women at age 60 were eligible for a state pension in Britain, and that my half-sister would be turning 60 in a few month's time and would likely apply for the pension. I waited until Margaret had passed her 60th birthday and then wrote again to the Department of Health and Social Security. After another wait I received their reply, returning my letter with their same form letter.

Our total lack of success in finding Margaret in Britain suggested that either we had been unable to unlock the key to her whereabouts in Britain or that she had left the country. If this was the case, there seemed to be no way in which I could find her. Then it occurred to me that Margaret's father might have left a will, and that this might contain some clue as to Margaret's whereabouts. The next time that I was in London I went to Somerset House. The first step in obtaining a will is to know, or find out the year of the person's death. I did not have this information, but could estimate it within a few years. I started at the latest year I thought her father would have died, and then worked backward year by year until I found his name. It read, 'Bernard Patrice Mahon of 48 Willoughby Road, London N.W.3. 9th June 1973. Probate London 11th September. £1481. Number 7301304738. Executor. Wife. Raimon Mahon.' To her he left £500. The residue he divided between his sister, Kathleen, and his daughter, Margaret. The will was duly witnessed and signed on 13 September 1969.

At last I had a possible opening to find Margaret through her stepmother, who was the executor of the will, and whose address was given, for she would have to have known Margaret's address in order to send her bequest. But what if Raimon Mahon had died! I went immediately to the nearest London phone book I could find, and to my joy her name was listed with the same address given in the will. Rather than phoning her, I decided to wait until I got home and then write to her. My letter was as follows:

Dear Mrs. Mahon,

I am a relative of the Wasley family and, like so many Americans, am interested in learning about the history of my family. There were four sisters: Mary, Teresa Gladys, Winifred and Lena. I believe that your step-daughter, Margaret, was the daughter of Teresa Gladys and I would like to get in touch with her. I would be most grateful to you if you could tell me where I can find her.

Sincerely, Stephen Richardson'

A month later I received a reply which read in part:

'I and my late husband married in 1942 – more than twelve years after the death of his first wife, Teresa Gladys. Their daughter had left school and was in her first job so I saw little of her and she never talked of her mother whom she lost as a small child and, obviously, scarcely remembered. My husband was much older than myself and all his family had died before him. I knew little of the Wasley family and lost touch with Margaret after her father's death. She was living in the US, but I do not remember her address and have no idea of her present whereabouts or, indeed, whether she is still alive. In any case, I am quite sure she would not know anything further.
I am so sorry that I cannot be of more help.

Sincerely yours, Vera R. Mahon

42

The letter explained why our earlier searches had been fruitless and told me what country I must now focus on if I were to continue looking for Margaret. I decided to write again to Vera Mahon and fully explain to her that Margaret was my half-sister, and that was the reason I so wanted to find her. Again, after sending the letter there was a wait of several weeks before I received a reply, which read in part:

> ...As I said before, I fear I have little more I can add to the information given in my previous letter except I can now give you Margaret's address. I got out all relevant papers and documents and can tell you that – at the time of my husband's death – she was married to a Mr. C (Charles?) Wadas and lived at 44 Humphrey Avenue, Bayonne, New Jersey. I was touched to read your story and hope these additional details may be of help...

At last I had something to go on, and I immediately phoned Information to see if she still lived at the same address. To my delight, there was a Wadas at the address that I had been given. My immediate response was to want to pick up the phone and call Margaret. On reflection, I decided that it would be wiser to write. I realized that if I were to establish a relationship with Margaret it would be that of an elder brother to a younger sister, with all the responsibilities that such a relationship entails – and this to someone whom I knew almost nothing about. I talked it over with my wife because it would involve her as well. She felt that I should go ahead and send her the letter. This I did.

The letter began, 'I believe that we are relatives. Let me tell you why, but first let me briefly introduce myself.' I told her of my adoption, and gave a brief autobiography and an account of my search for my biological family. I told her how I had found her address and how much I would like to meet her, and finished the letter with, 'I will

43

phone you in a few days after you have received this letter and look forward to talking with you and, if you would like, meeting you.' With the letter I enclosed copies of her and my birth certificates, which showed that we had the same mother.

In the days of waiting before phoning Margaret I reflected on my amazing good luck that Margaret and her stepmother had remained at the same addresses since Bernard Mahon's death in 1973, a 13-year period. If either had moved during that time I would probably never have found Margaret. During the years I had been searching in England, Margaret had been living just over an hour's drive away from my home in Connecticut. I wrote to Betty Birtwhistle and gave her the good news.

When I finally phoned Margaret, she told me that her husband had died and that she would like to meet me. We arranged a meeting at a restaurant near where she lived. I said that I would like to bring my wife, and she was agreeable to this.

Since I had first learned that I had a half-sister it had taken two years and eight months to find and meet her. My wife and I drove to our appointment with Margaret at the restaurant and on the way took a wrong turn, and arrived nearly half an hour late, fearful that she would not have waited for us. As we entered the restaurant we stopped and looked around to see if there was someone who might resemble family members of whom I had photographs. As we were looking, Margaret came up to us, guessing who we were, and so we finally met.

It was not apparent from our appearances that we were related. Margaret is five feet six inches tall and stockily built, whereas I am over six feet and thin. Margaret did not look like our mother, or other Wasley family members. Her build bore some resemblance to our oldest aunt's and our grandmother's, whereas I resemble my grandfather, and to some extent, our mother. We greeted each other warmly and, after I apologized for being late found a table in a quiet part of the restaurant.

44

It was a difficult situation for Margaret, and it took some time before she relaxed and began to tell us something about herself. She had had a very unhappy childhood. The only thing that she could remember about our mother was being taken to see her when she was in the hospice with terminal cancer. Our mother told her that all she wanted was to die. After her death she was sent to a Catholic boarding school, and at the end of each term, when all the other girls went home, she stayed at the school and was cared for by the nuns. She was very unhappy. When she left school she did nursing work in London, and was there during the worst of the bombing during World War Two.

She had almost no childhood memories of her father, who married a second time when Margaret was 17 years old. The marriage certificate showed that Margaret was a witness to his second marriage, but she had no memory of this event. From both Margaret and from her stepmother, whom I later met, I learned that their relationship was not a happy one. While working at a hospital she fell in love with a doctor who, after the war, emigrated to South Africa. Margaret followed him as soon as she could get a berth on a ship, and they got married. After a brief and very happy marriage her husband learned that he had cancer and committed suicide. Shortly after, she married an American naval seaman she met in South Africa, and he was then transferred to Germany. The marriage did not work out, and they were divorced. Margaret then came to the United States and supported herself in a number of jobs until she became an air hostess. While doing this work she met a flight engineer who flew for the same airline, and eventually they were married. The marriage lasted nearly 30 years, until her husband died after a long and debilitating illness through which she nursed him. They had no children. Her husband was brought up in a Polish family who wanted him to marry a good Polish girl, and Margaret felt very isolated from her in-laws, and after her husband died, felt very alone in the world without any relatives. Her father had died, and some years before we met her she had gone back to England and nursed him through his final illness. Our meeting with Margaret was two to three years after her husband had died. Shortly after our first get-together, we invited her to come and stay with us at Thanksgiving, and meet our children and grandchildren as a first step to becoming a member of the family.

I had been hoping that by finding Margaret I would learn from her more about our mother. As we got to know each other better, I would at different times press her gently to tell me more about her childhood and memories of our mother. She seemed to have almost completely wiped out any memories that preceded her leaving England as a young woman. Clearly, she had experienced a very unhappy childhood, but I thought she would have had more memories than she appeared to have. I read an article in the *New York Times* entitled 'In Memory, People Recreate Their Lives To Suit their Images of the Present' (23 June, 1987) that helped explain my puzzlement. It reviewed studies of memory, including one of 310 children who had had very troubled early lives. The researchers tracked down these children 30 years later, and discovered that those who had adjusted well in adulthood had fewer memories of the painful events of childhood than those who were currently suffering from emotional problems. Another study found that depressed people, for example, remember sad events from the past more easily than happy people, while the latter recall more pleasant moments. These studies suggest that Margaret's ability to cope as an adult was made easier by her forgetting her unhappy and difficult childhood.

8

Learning About Aunt Mary

It was clear from all that I had learned that, of my
mother's three sisters, Aunt Mary had been closest to my
mother and would know most about her. It was Aunt
Mary to whom my mother had gone when I was born,
and she had been my godmother when I was christened. If
I could find her, there would be so much she could tell me
about my mother and probably also something about my
father. Because I did not know the name of Mary's second
husband, I had been unable to obtain information from
the Register of Births, Marriages and Deaths. It was only
after I met Aunt Lena that she told me that Mary had
married a George Byfield and was dead. I regretted that I
had not started my search early enough to have met Aunt
Mary, but hoped that if I could find some of her children
that they would know something about my mother
through having met her, or been told about her from their
mother.

From the record offices at St Catherine's House and
Somerset House I found that Mary had married George
Byfield in 1962 at Harrow, near London, when she was 71
and George was 84. Ten years later George died, and Mary
died two years later in 1974, aged 84. The clue to finding
her children lay in her will. This showed that she died at
Glengarrif, Lower Claverham, near Bristol, and left her
estate to her son, Peter Mason. It was 13 years after Mary
had died when I found her will. From the phone book of
the Bristol area I found six Peter Masons listed, but none
of them lived at the address shown in the will. I sent the

same letter to each of them, explaining why I was trying to find the son of Mary Byfield, and giving some information about her. After what seemed a long wait two letters arrived saying that they were sorry, but they were not the Peter Mason that I was looking for. Then the following letter arrived:

Dear Mr Richardson,

We had a telephone call from the local farmer last Friday from whom we used to rent the bungalow called 'Glengariff'. I must say that we were very surprised to learn of a cousin in the States. My husband is, in fact, the person you are looking for. He was a pig farmer where we previously resided in Claverham, but put the farm up for sale five years ago as we had been making a loss for three years. We only managed to sell it two years ago as of course nobody wants to buy a pig farm. Most of our pork and bacon now seems to come from Denmark!

Excuse my typing this letter, but I work full-time and Peter never writes letters – even to his brothers/ sisters. Indeed, Peter's Mother was living with us when she died. About two years prior to her death she had lived in a flat over a shop that we ran and then when we sold the shop she came to live with us until she could move into an old persons flat nearby. In fact she was just about to move when she died.

Peter has two brothers in Australia – Stan and Ron. Fred lived in South Africa and died last year. Brian married a girl from Switzerland but none of the family have heard from him for years. Peter's sister, Barbara, who lives in Johannesburg, is the only one we regularly correspond with and she gives us information about all the family. Ron is very ill in hospital. Peter would dearly like to see him as I think it must be twenty years since they last met.

We never met the rest of your biological family. In

fact, quite a few years ago Peter took me to Yorkshire and we saw what remained of the house where he was born. So, we would like to hear about them. I have a case of Mrs Byfield's old photographs and think I possibly have a photograph of your mother. I presume that she is now dead and that you never have had contact with her.

I am so sorry that we did not meet you when you visited England last November. Please let us know if you ever come this way again. I did once visit the West coast of USA about seven years ago.

Hope to hear from you again.

Yours sincerely,

Peter and Pauline Mason

I was excited to at last have made contact with Aunt Mary's son, and looked forward to meeting Peter and Pauline. I hoped that the case of my aunt's photographs might help me learn about the Wasley family, and that from Peter and Pauline I would gain some picture of Aunt Mary.

The following summer I attended a conference in Dublin with my wife and afterwards arranged to visit Peter and Pauline, who had invited us to stay with them. We flew from Dublin to Bristol, where they wrote to say that they would meet us when our plane arrived. We were somewhat concerned that we might miss them because we had not arranged any way we would recognize each other.

There was a crowd waiting to meet people when we arrived, and without any hesitation my wife picked out Peter (see Fig 4). The similarity in our appearances was striking. Just as quickly they picked me out. They drove us to their home, which is a bungalow with a back garden that backs onto a large open field. We stayed with them for two days, and they took us to see some of the sights of Bristol. I talked at length with Peter about his family, learned more about his mother, his own history and about his brothers and sister, but he had never met my mother and knew nothing about her.

(Some years later he and his wife stayed with us in the USA and he read a draft of part of this manuscript. He then remembered an incident at his family's farm in Yorkshire, when he was a small boy. They were in the midst of harvesting, when the whole family worked long hours without stopping. One day, to Peter's great surprise, the work all stopped in order to welcome a woman visitor. He is sure that the woman must have been my mother.)

We greatly enjoyed our stay with Peter and Pauline, and found them so congenial that we have had several subsequent visits to them.

On our first visit they showed us the box of photographs which Pauline had mentioned in her letter. It was made of mahogany with brass corners, and on the hinged lid was a brass plate engraved with, 'Patrick Campion, Sergeant-Major'. This was my great-grandfather and Mary's grandfather.

Among the photos, I was delighted to at last be able to see Aunt Mary. There was a portrait of her taken when she was in her sixties or seventies, in which she gives the impression of strength and kindliness, with deep-set eyes looking directly at you, a touch of a smile and well-formed facial features. She is handsome rather than beautiful, and has a relaxed and watchful expression. Her build is heavy, but not fat. She is wearing a herringbone tweed dress. Another photo, taken at about the same time, shows her on holiday with a friend. The photograph albums of Aunt Winifred were not started until my aunts were adults, but in the box at Peter's house there were earlier photos of Wasley family members, including my mother and her sisters as children.

Peter's sister Barbara might know something about my mother, but she was living in South Africa. Pauline had written to her, telling her about me, and I wrote to Barbara, introducing myself and my search and asking if could tell me anything about my mother.

In her reply she wrote:

I am sorry that I never knew that Aunt Gladys had a
son. My mother never mentioned anything about that.
I cannot ever remember having seen your mother,
Stephen, neither did I meet Aunt Winifred and Lena.
My mother always spoke about them and I saw photographs of Winifred but, as far as I know, they never
ever came to visit us. My mother always said that her
parents would have nothing to do with her because
she married a farm labourer so you see Stephen I
never ever met my grandparents. I suppose they
thought my mother married beneath her standing.

Barbara wrote about her mother:

My mother was the most wonderful person, Stephen,
and I loved her very much. We were parted during the
war and afterwards when I was married. But we used
to see each other every Easter. Then of course we
came to South Africa. One does not think at the time
how much you can hurt your parents leaving them
behind, it is only when your own children have gone
away and you feel the sorrow that you understand
what you did to your own mother.

This sentence struck home to me, because I had left my
adoptive parents' home in Scotland when I was 26 and
emigrated to the United States.

The same year that Barbara first wrote to me she returned
to England, and we arranged to meet when my train arrived
at Burton on Trent. She was waiting for me on the platform
and immediately recognized me. We spent the day together
at the house of a friend of hers with whom she was staying,
and the friend kindly invited me to stay with them overnight.
Peter and his wife and Barbara treated me with such affection and kindness that I was deeply touched, and I felt the
same warm feelings for them. Barbara later wrote to Peter

51

and Pauline about the meeting, saying that looking into my eyes she could only think of her mother.

Barbara is almost six feet in height, with broad shoulders and a powerful build (see Fig 5). After she left school around the age of 14, Barbara went to work in a jewellers' shop at Skipton; then her mother had a heart attack, and Barbara had to stay home to look after her until she recovered. World War Two was in progress, and young women had to do war work. Barbara chose to work at a canteen at a large naval base and then joined the ATS, the women's branch of the Army, and worked on gun sites in England, France and Germany. They lived in metal huts at the gun sites with no running water, heat or electricity. Water was delivered by a truck. It was intensely cold in winter, and to keep warm she always slept in her clothes. When they went on leave, the first thing they looked for was a hot bath.

After the end of the War in Europe, Barbara transferred to the Military Police. During the Nuremberg war criminal trials she escorted women who were on trial between the prison and the court room, and stood behind the prisoners in the court room throughout the trials. She met her future husband in Germany, where he was driving a truck which transported the prisoners to the trials. After their war service ended, Barbara and her husband returned to England and her husband resumed his work as a carpenter. After their first child was born, Barbara contracted tuberculosis and was hospitalized for over a year. After her recovery, they had five more children.

Feeling that South Africa would provide more opportunity for their children than England, they emigrated there. Two years after they had moved, Barbara's husband died of cancer and she was left with six children. The Anglican church came to her aid and placed her boys in one of their boys' homes, St George's. It was about half an hour's trip away from where Barbara lived. On weekends the boys would come back to her from the home. The whole village where they had lived in England rallied round and sent them a collection of money. Her eldest brother paid the mortgage on the house, and the South African Legion sent them money for food. Barbara worked taking in boarders, baking and sewing. There was no governmental assistance. After the boys finally left the school they went into various trades. Since meeting Barbara, I have kept in touch through correspondence.

9

The Search For My Father

Even a cursory inspection of this book will show that it deals predominantly with my birth mother and her family, and the reader may well wonder about my father. To satisfy such curiosity, I am including my search for him early in the story, even though by doing so I may somewhat interrupt the overall flow.

My search for my birth parents had so far succeeded in the identification of my mother and enough information about her and her family to continue exploring their histories. By contrast, my attempts to find my father had all been fruitless. His name and occupation were blanks on my birth certificate. Later, I found out that even if my mother had wished to fill in these blanks, she was prohibited by law, which required the presence of my father when the birth was registered, if my mother was not married.

The other information I had obtained, or surmised, turned out to be false. My father was not the chauffeur of the titled family in Yorkshire, as my adoptive aunt had told me, and was not a member of that family. Neither of my aunts, Winifred or Lena, had any knowledge of my existence until I turned up, so they did not know. I later learned that Winifred may have known. In a letter to Lena, telling about my first contact with her, she wrote, 'So Gladys' secret is out.' This suggests that she may have known or suspected that there was a child. My mother had been very close to her elder sister, Mary, and would probably have confided in her, but she was dead and her two children, whom I met, had not been told by their mother.

There seemed no way I could learn about my father, until a possible path opened up when I was speaking to a senior official at the Register of Births, Marriages and Deaths. He told me that adoption agencies would require the names of both birth parents and some information about each of them as part of the record of the adoption. This started me off on a search to find out the agency through which I was adopted. This information was not on my adoption certificate. Initially, I thought of two ways of going about the search: one was to see whether the records of the court that officiated over my adoption would have the information I sought (I had their address on my adoption certificate); the other would be to find the agency through which I was adopted and ask them to share with me their records of the adoption.

In seeking the court records of my adoption I immediately ran into a legal obstacle. This was explained in a pamphlet, *Access to Birth Records*, issued by the office for National Statistics, which gives the background for adoptions in England and Wales:

> In the past it was thought better for all concerned that an adopted child's break with his birth family should be total. Parents who placed a child for adoption were generally told that a child would not have access to his birth record. The current legislation reflects increased understanding of the wishes and needs of adopted people. It recognizes that although adoption makes a child a full member of a new family, information about his or her origins may still be important to an adopted person.
>
> People adopted before 12 November 1975 are required to see a counsellor before they can be given access to their records because in the years before 1975, some parents and adopters may have been led to believe that the children being adopted would never be able to find out their original names or the names of their parents. These arrangements were

made in good faith and it is important that adopted people who want to find out more about their origins should understand what it may mean for them and for others.

This means that if you were adopted before 12 November 1975, the adoption act requires you to see an experienced social worker, called a counsellor, before you can obtain information from your original birth record.

I learned that such a counsellor could give me authority to obtain from the court which made the adoption legal, the name of the agency which arranged the adoption. Mine was an odd situation, because I already had my birth certificate and knew a considerable amount about my mother and her family.

I made an appointment with an official at the National Register Office in London, and explained my situation and why I needed a court order. He was sympathetic and gave me the court order I needed to pursue my enquiry.

I could now comply with the legal requirement of having a court order from a counsellor, so I wrote to the court through which I was officially adopted. They replied that they had no record of my adoption and suggested that I contact the Greater London Council at their record office and history library. I then received the suggestion that the records I was seeking might be obtained from the Archivist at the Greater London Records office.

I wrote to them, and they replied that the strongroom holding their records was sealed off because of the removal of asbestos. This work would take some time and there had been an accumulation of enquiries, so there would be a long delay before they could deal with my request. Several months later they wrote again that their office only had records for children in care between 1931–65. They passed on my request to another office of the Corporation of London, which had earlier records, and in time they wrote saying that they had found no record of my adoption. At this point I decided that there was no point in continuing this path of enquiry.

Prior to the adoption act of 1927, a source of finding children available for adoption was family doctors, who would know of a child needing adoption, find someone who wanted a child and then arrange the transfer of the child. I doubted whether this had occurred in my case, because I knew where my adoptive parents and my birth mother had lived around 1920, and their residences had been too far apart for them to have had access to the same doctors.

To make a search of agencies from which I might have been adopted, I needed a comprehensive list of them. This I obtained from 'British Agencies for Adoption and Fostering' at 11 Southwark Street in London, in a publication entitled *Where to Find Adoption Records*. I went to the office and spoke to the author of the list, Georgina Stafford, a social worker with whom I later corresponded over the years, and who gave me much helpful advice.

The book listed hundreds of agencies, and I needed some way of selecting the ones I should contact. Because my mother was a Catholic, it would be likely that she would choose a Catholic agency. It was also likely that my adoptive parents would go to an agency near to where they were living. They had moved to London in 1920. The earliest photograph that I have of myself was as an infant in a pram, taken in the garden of our London house when I was about nine months old. The adoption must have taken place sometime between late 1920 and early 1921. My adoptive parents, prior to coming to London, had lived in Manchester, so it was possible that through their contacts in Manchester, the adoption had taken place there. With this knowledge, I looked up Catholic agencies in London and Manchester. They searched their files without success, and in their replies suggested other Catholic agencies. When I wrote to the Catholic Children's Society, I told them my adoptive aunt's story that my mother wanted me to be adopted into a Catholic family,

57

but not finding such a family, the agency had allowed a Quaker family to adopt me.

In a reply from the Catholic Children's Society, which had no record of me, they wrote:

> I think that I can say with some confidence that no Catholic Agency would have placed you in the care of non-Catholic parents in those days – you would have remained in residential care if a family could not be found from within the Catholic community. This would have been considered preferable than the risk of your losing the faith, which was the prime concern of Rescue Societies of the time.

On a visit to Manchester with my wife, we visited the Franciscan Missionaries of St Joseph, a Catholic order whose activities included arranging adoptions. My wife told one of the Sisters about my search and gave them the information they needed to see if they had taken me in as a baby. They looked into the matter for us, and we paid them a second visit. They were unable to find any record of me, and in the ensuing conversation they told us that their organization would never have let me be adopted by parents who were not Catholic. If no Catholic parents could be found, they would have kept me in an orphanage. At the time I was born there was competition for children between the Catholic church and Barnardo's, a large organization that looked after children and arranged for adoptions without regard for the religion of the birth parents. They also told us that in 1920 to be an unmarried mother was a mark of severe stigma, and that to have a baby out of wedlock was something that the mother would keep as secret as possible.

From what I had learned, I stopped writing to Catholic agencies and chose non-Catholic and nonsectarian agencies in London and Manchester. In all, I wrote to over a dozen, and each replied that they had no record, and would sometimes suggest other places to try.

58

Fig 1 Gladys Wasley (page 18)

Cousins I met
Children of Lena and Bernard Elliman

Fig 2
Joanna Leathert,
daughter of Lena, sister
of Jonathan (page 34)

Fig 3
Jonathan Elliman, son of
Lena, brother of Joanna
(page 36)

Cousins I met
Children of Mary and Walter Mason

Fig 4
Peter Mason, son of
Mary, brother of
Barbara (page 49)

Fig 5
Barbara, daughter of
Mary, sister of Peter
(page 52)

Fig 6
Tower Cressy,
Aubrey Road, London.
House from where I w.
adopted (page 62)

Fig 7
Patrick Campion, my
great grandfather
(page 72)

Fig 8 My grandmother, Sarah Campion Wasley, Frank Wasley's wife (page 72)

Fig 9 My grandfather,
Frank Stephen Wasley (page 77)

Fig 10 My grandfather,
Frank Stephen Wasley (page 78)

Fig 11 My mother (left) with her mother Sarah
and sisters Winifred and Mary (page 77)

Fig 12
My mother with her
elder sister Mary
(page 78)

Fig 13 My mother (left) with sister Lena and Father 1924 (page 78)

Fig 14 Winifred (page 89)

Fig 15 Lena (left), Winifred and my half-sister Margaret (Peggy) (page 90)

Fig 16
At Henley
(left to right)
Lena, Winifred, my mother
(page 101)

Fig 17 My mother at Courtland Farm,
Horsham, Sussex (page 101)

Fig 18 My mother with Peggy
(page 106)

I had just about given up the search when I visited my adoptive cousin, Peggy Jay, and told her about my search. To my surprise, she told me that she remembered going with her mother and my adoptive mother when they chose me at a large private house somewhere around Kensington in London. It did not look like an institution. There were several infants in a playpen, wearing leggings and a white smock, and I was standing up, holding on to the playpen, but unable to walk. I was chosen, and it was like picking a puppy out of a litter. At the time, my cousin was seven to eight years old. This was the best clue I had obtained since my search began. I could now focus on West London as the location of the adoption, and on a private house rather than an institutional structure.

My adoptive parents, in looking for an adoption agency, would probably have turned to what written information on the subject was available at the time. Someone suggested that the best place now to look for such information was the Library of the City of London, which is located at Brewers' Hall Garden, EC2V 5BX. When next in London I went there, told the Reference Librarian what I was looking for, and asked her for her advice. She suggested the Post Office Directory of 1920, and I obtained a copy and found a desk in a quiet corner. It gave the addresses of several of the agencies to which I had already written and received negative replies. The Librarian then suggested the *Annual Charities Register and Digest*, but they did not have the 1920 edition; my time was limited, and I had to leave.

From the preface to *Where to find Adoption Records* I learned that a complete set of the *Charities Register and Digest* was to be found at the British Library. This was housed at the British Museum, which I visited on my next trip to England.

At an anteroom to the Library and Reading Room I was told to look up the reference number to the publication on a computer. First I had to convince the staff that other libraries did not have the book. Having accepted my explanation, they asked me to fill out forms. They told me, after inquiry, that it would be retrieved from storage the following day, and that I should phone to check whether the books had arrived. Then I was photographed and given a reader's card with the photo made valid for one year, so that I could use the library. This required more forms to be filled in.

On the following day I phoned the library, and was told that the books might be available later and I was to phone again at 3.00 p.m. This I did, and was told the books had arrived from their storage. So I hurried over, and with a feeling of some self-importance, showed my newly acquired pass and was admitted to the main Reading Room.

I was awestruck by the size and magnificence of the room and the history of those who had used the room. It was circular in shape, with a great hemispherical dome painted in light blue with windows all around and a large skylight at the summit of the dome. The walls below the dome were about 40 feet high, with two galleries, and completely lined with books. Reading desks were arranged like the spokes of a wheel, and in the centre was a desk where officials dealt with enquiries. Many of the desks were occupied with readers, each with an array of books and documents and, a recent change, a majority using laptop computers.

A studious silence hung over the room, which had been built about 150 years ago. It had a great history of learning and had been occupied by so many great men in search of information – authors including Kipling, Bernard Shaw, E.M. Forster, Hardy, Dickens and Darwin, and world figures such as Marx, Ma73
hatma Gandhi and Sun Yat-sen, father of the Chinese Republic. For awhile, I almost forgot why I had come to this place. I was fortunate to have had this visit, because the room has since been closed and the British Library is now housed in a new building near St Pancras station.

I was directed through a door and corridor that led to the North Reading Room where at a desk I obtained the

1920 and 1921 *Charities Registers* I had ordered. They asked me what reading station I would occupy, so I found a quiet spot up on a balcony, gave them the number and settled down to read.

The *Charities Register* table of contents had a section for children, and I went through all the listed entries. Some of the subheadings listed I found were not relevant, such as 'Relief in Distress (Permanent)'. These all were orphanages of different kinds that took older boys and trained them for various vocations. 'Homes for Boys and Girls' – many of these only took in special categories of orphans, such as children of 'clergymen, officers and professional men', or 'orphans of Seamen' or 'children who had been ill treated'. Again, these kept the young people throughout their childhood.

In the entire section on children there was only a single reference to adoption. This was:

'National Children Adoption Association, 19 Sloane Street, SW1; Hostel, Tower Cressy, Aubrey Road, W. *Object* – The promotion of the adoption of children and the maintenance of a Nursery Training School for educated girls.'

This agency was listed in the 1920 and 1921 editions, and in the 1921 edition there was a half-page at the beginning under the heading of 'Charities Register Advertiser', giving more or less the same information as shown above.

It was reasonable that my adoptive parents would have used the *Charities Register* and picked out the only adoption agency. The Children's Adoption Association appeared then to be the place from which I was adopted. Several agencies specified the religious background as a condition of entry, but no such statement appeared for the Children's Adoption Association.

I decided on my next and last morning in England to go and look for the house Tower Cressy at Aubrey Road W. A street map showed it was near Holland Park in South

Kensington, where my adoptive cousin, Peggy Jay, remembered visiting. The street was quite steep, with fairly small houses with numbers, not names. At the top of the street were two large houses with names, but not the name of Tower Cressy. I went to one of the large houses and they knew nothing of Tower Cressy, but said part of their house had been damaged by bombs in World War Two. At the second house I found an elderly man who told me Tower Cressy had been across the road, but had been destroyed by bombs in the War. New smaller houses were now standing on the site.

To see if I could learn more about the house I went to the Kensington Town Hall and the Town Planning Office. All they could tell me was that planning permission was given in 1957 for building new houses on the site of Tower Cressy. They suggested I go to the Town Library next door, where I found a section and reference librarian who dealt with town history. She knew of the house of Tower Cressy and pulled out a photo and a drawing of the house (see Fig 6).

She showed me a book that gave the information that the house was built in 1852–53 for Thomas Page, the engineer who designed Waterloo Bridge. It was damaged during World War Two and demolished shortly afterwards. They had no further information.

On my list of things to explore on this trip was the National Adoption Society, where I went after investigating Tower Cressy – I went because I could find no phone for them. At the office, when I explained to the receptionist why I had come, she told someone in the office about my visit.

This person then spoke to me by phone and said she did not deal with adoption records. She also said that the National Children's Adoption Society, which I had come to, was often confused with the National Children Adoption Association. I had been confused. The person who dealt with adoptions only came in on Mondays, and she gave me her name and address and said that I should write to her. She also told me that the National Children

Adoption Association did have adoption records from the 1920s. It was very exciting to know that at last I might be able to get the records of my adoption. It was time to go out to the airport, but I just had time to send a short note to my cousin who had gone with my adoptive mother to Cressy Towers, to ask her whether the copy of the picture of the house that I enclosed in the letter was the one that she had been to. Later she replied that the picture looked the same as her memory of the house. This increased my confidence that, at last, I had found where I had been adopted.

As soon as I got home, I wrote to the office where the City of Westminster Department of Social Services, London, kept the records of the National Children Adoption Association, giving my history and why I wanted to know about my adoption. They acknowledged my letter, writing that 'The matter is currently receiving attention and we will be contacting you again as soon as possible.' I then had to wait nearly two months before I heard from them again. In writing this account of my search for the agency through which I was adopted, I have telescoped this history into a few pages, which makes it seem that it happened over a relatively short period of time. In fact, from the time I wrote the first letter about my adoption until ~~what~~ I finally found what I was looking for spanned a time period of 13 years.

The day came when I received a fat envelope from the City of Westminster, and from its bulk I immediately guessed that they had found something. I opened the envelope and first read their letter. They wrote:

Sadly, as you are well aware, it is not easy to trace reliable information on places, people and events after so many years. At the time your adoption was being arranged and, in fact, for a great many years afterwards, the importance and significance of personal roots was not appreciated and adopted people were denied relevant knowledge. In a great many cases of pre-war adoptions no records were kept or else they were destroyed during the war.

However, we have succeeded in finding one document relating to your adoption, a copy of which I enclose.

They also sent some information taken from the NCAA's annual report of 1923/4, which gives information about how the organization functioned. I turned to the document to which the letter referred. It was called an indenture and recorded the transfer of my legal guardianship from my birth mother to my adoptive mother. There was no information about my father. After such a long search, this was a deep disappointment.

I had given up hope of ever learning anything about my biological father, until suddenly a new clue gave me some hope. On a visit to my aunt, Lena was talking about her early history when she suddenly changed topic and said, 'You know that your mother was very fond of an Australian serviceman that she met at a canteen after the war.' (World War One). My wife was with me, and after our visit she recalled that the middle name given me by my birth mother was Sydney. The spelling was the same as the city in Australia and not, as was generally used, for a person's name, where the spelling would be Sidney. Perhaps my mother was trying to tell me something.

Later, I remembered that my adoptive aunt who had given me the incorrect information about my parentage had also told me a story about my brother's biological parents. My brother was three years older than I, and had also been adopted. Her story was that my brother's father was a Private in the Australian army and that his mother was a domestic servant. It seemed incredible that both my brother and I should have parents of the same background, and it seemed far more likely that somehow my adoptive aunt had got the stories of our parentage mixed up, and that the story ascribed to my brother was really the story about me. I wrote to the National Register of Births,

Marriages and Deaths asking for a copy of my brother's birth certificate to see if I could confirm my adoptive aunt's mix-up, but they replied that they were prohibited by law from giving me a copy of the birth certificate.

Some time later, I spent some time in Henley and found time to go through the 1919 files of the local paper to see if there were any references to Australian servicemen in the vicinity of Henley, which is where my mother was living at that time. A 25 July heading of 'Canteen' seized my attention. The article was a description of a canteen for servicemen and was part of a peace celebration at Wargrave, near Henley. The volunteers who planned the canteen gave out over 400 coupons to service people that they used to obtain food and drink, including 1,500 sandwiches which the volunteers had prepared. After the food, there was a band and dancing. I wondered if that was where my mother had met the Australian. The only reference to Australians in the newspaper was in a description of the Royal Henley Peace Regatta. Among the competitors were two eight-oared crews, two four-oared crews and a sculler, who were all Australian servicemen. One of the crews won the King's Cup by defeating the Oxford University Service Crew. Could my father have been an oarsman? (Maybe this was wishful thinking because I compete in rowing regattas.)

I wrote to the headquarters of the Henley Regatta, asking if they had the names of those who rowed in 1919. Thy sent me a 16-page report of the 1919 Royal Henley Peace Regatta, which included the names of all the oarsmen. My hope had been that they would give the full names so that I could see if any of them had a Christian name of Sydney. Unfortunately, only surnames and initials of Christian names were given. One Australian had an 'S' initial and his rank was Major. My adoptive aunt had said the Australian she mentioned as my brother's father was a Private. I felt the Henley clue was too slim to warrant further pursuit.

I made several other attempts to try and establish

whether there had been Australian servicemen stationed around the Henley area in 1919 by writing to the National Army Museum and the Imperial War Museum. Neither of them had the information that I sought. I then went to Australia House in London, and after telling the receptionist why I had come, was shown into a waiting room that had a telephone on the desk. After waiting awhile, the telephone rang and my enquiry was dealt with by phone rather than on a face-to-face basis. This arrangement had happened to me once before in London, and I wondered whether this arrangement had been thought up by some efficiency expert as a way of reducing the time taken to answer enquiries. I did not like the phone arrangement. However, the man at the other end of the phone heard me out and then told me that he had been adopted as a child and had been able to find his biological father in Australia. He suggested that I write to the Australian War Memorial Research Centre in Canberra, where there are extensive documentary sources on past wars. When I got home, I followed his suggestion and in a reply learned that all information was classified by individual names.

I talked to a friend who came from Australia and told him about my search. He told me that his grandfather had been in the Australian forces in World War One, and after the war had been in London in 1919, obtaining some training for civilian work. He was interested in rowing and had gone to Henley to watch the 1919 regatta. He showed me a book about the history of his grandfather's regiment. After the war they had been in England, and they had sailed for Australia in August of 1919. If all the regiments had histories written about them, this might help me learn whether some regiment was stationed in the vicinity of Henley in September 1919, when I was conceived. If my mother gave me the name of Sydney because it was my father's name, this might also be a possible clue.

After several more enquiries in Australia, I sadly concluded that it would be fruitless to go any further without the name of my father. It left me wondering what happened to him after I was born and why he apparently disappeared from my mother's life. As a war veteran, it is likely that he and his regiment were shipped back to Australia, and this may have occurred early in my mother's pregnancy. She may have tried to get in touch in Australia, or perhaps decided not to tell him of the pregnancy.

10

The Early Lives of My Mother's Parents

In trying to learn about the history of my grandparents, I was able to learn far more about my grandfather. As has been so often the case in the lives of men and women in the late nineteenth and early twentieth century, men had more choice and freedom in developing their lives than women, whose roles were generally prescribed and limited by society to marriage, homemaking and bearing and raising children.

My grandfather, Frank Stephen Wasley, was, according to his birth certificate, born in Peckham in south-east London in 1848. His father's occupation is given as 'Parliamentary Clerk'. The only reference to his childhood I could find was in an article in *The Artist*, published in 1901: 'He revelled in long solitary rambles in the country.' When Frank was 22, he married Clara Edith Lee, aged 19, who came from Liverpool; the wedding certificate shows that her father was a tea merchant. Under occupation, Frank entered 'Gentleman', rather than 'Musician'. This may be an early indication of the importance that he attached to his social status. His wife's occupation was given as 'Spinster'. Frank was brought up as a Roman Catholic, and I was surprised that the marriage certificate shows that the ceremony took place according to the rites and ceremonies of the Wesleyan Methodists. It took place in West Derby, Lancashire.

About a year later, in 1871–72, Frank and his wife, Clara, went to Canada, where they remained for about four years. Aunt Winifred and the article in *The Artist* indicated that he went on a concert tour as a pianist. Aunt Lena told me that when they arrived in Canada, Clara's trunks, with her clothes, were stolen, and Frank had a cello which was also stolen. Later I learned that he also played the violin. This information was on Clara's death certificate, where she gave as Frank's occupation, 'Musician – violin'. They went to Saskatchewan as homesteaders and built a log cabin. Frank travelled around by horse and cart, tuning pianos and performing on the piano and violin. Lena told me that he put bells on the harness of the horse to keep off the wolves. At some time during their stay their log cabin burned down. If he had gone on a concert tour of Canada as Winifred had told me, it might be expected that this would have been in the main cities in the eastern part of Canada, and that it would not have lasted four years.

Apart from what Lena told me, I have no information about Frank's and Clara's lives in Saskatchewan. However, we may be able to infer something about their lives from the history of the time and place. At the time Frank went to Canada, Saskatchewan was sparsely populated and not yet a province of Canada. To encourage settlement in the West, 160-acre homesteads were offered free to immigrants from Europe, and the attractive aspects of being a homesteader were probably emphasized. Financial assistance was available from both governmental and private sources. These conditions may have influenced the Wasleys' decision to go west. When they arrived in Canada there was only a trickle of immigrants compared to the flood that came later. The temperatures in Saskatchewan show extremes of summer heat and winter cold, with average temperatures in January being around 0 degrees fahrenheit. George Brown in his book, *Building the Canadian Nation*, writes of that time:

For the first pioneer families life was hard and often drab. The burdens of work left time for little else, and separation from neighbors often brought a feeling of loneliness and isolation.

Churches and schools were the community centres not only for education and religion, but also for entertainment and recreation. On the frontier people might gather in a house or in the open air. The area where the Wasleys homesteaded cannot have been too isolated or primitive, because Frank drove around tuning pianos and possibly playing at gatherings. Whether his skills with music provided him with a living and to what extent he did some farming we do not know.

The years that the Wasleys were in Saskatchewan in the 1870s were a period of change and unrest in that part of Canada. Many native Americans were starving because of the disappearance of the buffalo herds. Their unrest led to the establishment of a Canadian Department of Indian Affairs. In 1870, a military expedition was sent west to prevent trouble, and it went to Fort Garry near where Winnipeg now stands. To get there required travelling over 300 miles through wilderness from the western end of Lake Superior, where there was no railway. To reach Saskatchewan, the Wasleys had a journey of 700 miles or more from the Great Lakes.

The only direct evidence that Frank lived in Canada comes from his sketchbooks. There is a sketch of the Canadian Rockies, so entitled, with a date that looks like 1875. There is a lake in the foreground, and forest and mountains in the background. Later, I found a charcoal drawing of Niagara Falls, suggesting that he was also there.

These show that Frank was already interested in art as well as music, and he may have travelled farther west than Saskatchewan before returning to England in 1875. Aunt Lena told me that Frank's wife, Clara, could no longer stand the life on the frontier, left him and came back to England late in 1874, pregnant with their first child, Edith.

From Clara's return to England about 1875 until her death in Liverpool in 1904, I was unable to learn anything about her. Aunt Lena thought that when she came back to England she had problems with alcohol, and chronic alcoholism was given as a cause of her death in her death certificate. The certificate stated that she was a widow of Frank Wasley, which is puzzling because at the time of her death, Frank was still alive. Further evidence suggesting that she had serious problems was the transfer of guardianship of her daughter, Edith, to Frank's sister and her husband, who brought her up from about the age of seven. Clara died intestate, and in the grant of administration Frank Wasley was assigned £107. 5s. 6d. There is an unexplained contradiction between this bequest and her being recorded as a widow.

After Frank's return to England in 1875 at the age of 27, I was able to learn little about his activities during the next 16 years. In an introduction to an exhibition of Frank's paintings it says that he moved on from pencil sketches to oil paintings. In the article in *The Artist* the author writes that when Frank returned from Canada 'he seriously determined to woo the sister art'. He was a self-taught artist and was influenced by Turner and Cox. In 1880, there is a reference to his being a black-and-white artist, and in 1881 at an exhibition of his paintings he made his first sale to the Walker Art Gallery in Liverpool of an oil painting entitled 'Evening on the Esk'.

Frank's art during this period provides some clues about where he lived and what he liked to portray in his pictures. From different sources I have been able to make a list of over 200 of his pictures, most of which gave the location and dates.

It is clear from the content of his pictures that marine subjects were his prime interest, and when the pictures were inland, rivers are nearly always prominent in the foreground. Very few of the pictures are of rural scenes where water is not present. Many of the marine pictures include sunrises and sunsets, storms at sea, sailing fishing boats in the open sea, making for, or leaving harbour, and fishermen at work on their boats. Some of the paintings show larger sailing ships as seen from the land. There are no pictures where the artist is aboard a ship. In the river scenes the background is frequently a castle, or abbey. Of the few pictures where there is no water, the scenes depicted are various. For example, 'Gypsy Encampment at Twilight', 'Horse and Cart in Winter Landscape', 'Rain at Sunset', 'A Country Lane'. In these pictures the sky is an important part of the composition. While Frank did a few portraits, the ones that I have seen are all privately owned and do not appear in any of the lists of sales. To me they are very lifelike, including a self-portrait and a sketch of his first child.

The locations showed that he spent time on the south coast of England in Sussex around the Brighton area, the southwest coast around Bristol, Dartmoor, Devon and Cornwall, and another set of pictures in Yorkshire, especially along the coast.

At age 42 in 1891, Frank married a second time, to Sarah Winfred Campion, aged 24 (see Fig 8). Her father, Patrick Campion, had been a Sergeant-Major in the army, and in his retirement was living in Bristol (see Fig 7). He and his wife Elizabeth had three daughters and a son who died young. Jonathan, Aunt Lena's son, found out that Patrick Campion, our great-grandfather, was in the Green Howards regiment, and he visited the regiment's museum in Yorkshire. The curator immediately recognized the name of Patrick Campion and found the following entry in the regimental gazette of September 1899:

We regret to record the death of a well-known Green Howard, Mr. Patrick Campion, who passed away on the 12th of August at his residence in Bristol. He joined the regiment in 1838 and with it served in Malta, the Ionian Islands, the West Indies, and Canada, returning to England in 1851. He was one of those who served throughout the whole of the Crimean campaign from its invasion, 14th September, 1854, till the fall of Sebastopol, 9th September, 1855.

72

He took part in the battles of the Alma and Inkerman, and was present at the storming of the Redan and the attack on the Quarries. At the Alma he earned the medal for distinguished conduct in the field, for his gallant rescue, in company with a couple of his comrades, of a wounded officer of his own company, who was lying in front of the Russian lines. In 1856 he returned to England as Sergeant-Major of the battalion, and with it went out to India at the close of the Mutiny. In 1860 he took his discharge, and the same year was appointed Sergeant-Major of the Bristol Rifles. Five years later his services in connection with the corps were recognized by a gift from the officers of a gold watch and 100 pounds. On his retirement from the corps in 1880, the past and present officers of the regiment presented him with a handsome silver cup, and a silver teapot for his wife, whilst the Sergeants gave him a marble clock. The funeral took place on the 16th of August, and was attended by many members of the Bristol Rifles, as well as several Crimean and Indian Mutiny veterans. A Union Jack was placed on the coffin, and also the deceased's sword, as well as the shako he wore when in the Green Howards.

Later, he sent my cousin the further information that Patrick was born in County Kilkenny in Ireland, and prior to being sworn into the army at age 19 was a farm labourer. He was six feet in height, strongly built, with a fresh complexion, grey eyes and brown hair. After he died, at some time Patrick Campion's medals came into the possession of my mother's eldest sister, Mary. She was hard up and sold the medals. The regiment heard about this and bought the medals, which are now on display in their museum.

The marriage certificate of Frank and Sarah shows the marriage was solemnized in the Roman Catholic Church of St Bede's in Manchester. Frank gives his condition as

'Widower' and Sarah as 'Spinster'. Frank gives his occupation as 'Marine Artist', rather than the designation he used as 'Gentleman' for his first marriage. They both gave the same address.

There are peculiar things about the information given. Frank describes himself as a widower, when we know from the death certificate of his first wife Clara that she was still alive at this time, and Edith, the daughter of Frank from his first marriage, was present as a witness at the ceremony. In the death certificate of Clara, the information given is that she is a widow when we know that Frank was alive.

How to explain this information is puzzling. If Frank's daughter had known that her mother was alive, it is highly unlikely that she would have acted as a witness to the second marriage. At the time she was 17 years old, and she had been brought up by Frank's sister and her husband. We do not know at what age Edith was separated from her mother and how the separation was explained to her. It is reasonable to assume that she had been told that her mother had died and that she had had no contact with her mother for many years. It is possible that her mother had been in some sort of institution because of her alcoholism, and that this information had been kept from her. This would have freed her to act as a witness to the marriage.

It is harder to explain why Frank put himself down as 'widower'. He must either have been lying, or had come to believe that his first wife was dead. In the eyes of the Catholic church, the first marriage may have been regarded as invalid, and if so, Frank might have claimed that he was a bachelor, rather than a widower. However, he could not do this with his daughter present as a witness. What is clear is that Frank's second marriage was bigamous in the eyes of the law.

There are two pieces of information that may throw some light on the puzzle of Frank's marriage. My Aunt Lena told me that Frank's first wife had eloped from her parents' family in order to get married. The birth certificate of their first-born child, Mary, shows that she was born between six and seven months after the marriage, so that it is likely that Frank and his wife knew of the pregnancy before they were married. If Frank had known that his first wife was still alive, but had kept this information to himself, he would then have been placed in the dilemma of having to decide whether to go ahead with the marriage and risk discovery of the bigamy, or to have not married Sarah, with the consequent shame and stigma that would fall on her. As it turned out, there is no indication that the bigamous nature of the marriage became known. If Frank had withheld this information from Sarah, it is likely that she learned about it when Frank received the bequest in her will from his first wife, 13 years after his second marriage. This occurred the same year that Frank and Sarah's youngest child, Lena, was born. One can only speculate how Sarah responded to this revelation.

11

The Childhood of My Mother and Her Family

My mother's father, Frank, was a major influence on his wife and children. At age 43 when he married Sarah, he had lived in England as a bachelor for 16 years, and his major interests were already well-established and would remain little changed for the rest of his life. They were his music, art, his love of fishing and the sea coast, ships, rivers and countryside that were the subjects that he chose to paint. These were primarily solitary pursuits, requiring little need for social and interpersonal relationships. He was always looking for new subjects to paint, and this caused him to keep moving from one place to another. For many years after his marriage he would find a location that he liked and then take a six-month tenancy in a furnished house, before moving on to another place and house.

Given these frequent moves, Sarah and the girls had little opportunity to develop friendships, and their circle of potential friends would have been restricted to persons of similar social class. The girls, especially the younger two, Winifred and Lena, had no continuity of schooling. As was probably customary in those days, Frank left the running of the household and care of the girls up to his wife, Sarah. At times, they were short of money, and this must have placed an additional burden on her. With four girls, the upkeep of the family's clothes must have been time-consuming, and would leave Sarah little time to develop and pursue any interests of her own.

Sarah was about five and a half feet tall. In the photo I have of her, aged 34, at Whitby with her children, she is sitting with her hands clasped, looking rather solemn and wearing a long dark dress with large lace bertha and high collar (see Fig 11). While Lena spoke often about her father she almost never mentioned her mother, and I regret that I did not ask Lena more about her. The two elder girls, Mary and my mother, in their later childhood were sent to a Catholic convent boarding school in Yorkshire, whereas the two younger girls stayed in their parents' home throughout their school years, with a short interlude at a boarding school for Lena, which ended at the outbreak of war.

Social class was a major influence on the lifestyles of the English during the life of the Wasley family, and its importance to Frank is suggested at the time of his first marriage, when he put down on his marriage certificate 'Gentleman' to describe his 'Rank, or profession'. By the time of his second marriage he wrote 'Marine Artist', indicating that he felt more secure and successful in his role as an artist. This occupation gave him upper social class status, but his income was dependent on his sale of pictures, had little stability, and may well have been lower than that expected for his social class. Respectability was an important element within social classes, and this meant being independent as well as exhibiting proper, socially acceptable behaviour. Every respectable man wanted to be a gentleman, and for Frank, respectability was very important.

The dress and appearance of the family were also indicators of social status, and it is clear from photographs of the family that Frank was well aware of this. The photos came from those collected by Mary Wasley and kept by her son, Peter, and the photograph albums of Winifred Wasley, which, after her death, were passed on to her sister, Lena. In a photo of Frank around 1907, when he was in his late fifties, he is seated on an artist's three-legged stool, holding a painting with an easel before him and his palette and brushes on the ground beside him (see Fig 9). He is carefully dressed in a suit with a stiff collar, a bow tie and a folded handkerchief sticking out of his breast pocket. In other photos taken when he was older, reading at home (see Fig 10), standing on the bridge at Henley, and out for a walk in the country (see Fig 13), the same careful attention to dress is shown. Studio photographs of the children taken around 1898 show how elaborately they were dressed. They wore huge leghorn hats tied on with ribbons and crowned with ostrich feathers. They are wearing long white dresses decorated with lace at the neck and sleeves (see Fig 12).

Jonathan, my biological first cousin, gave me a walking stick that had belonged to our grandfather, Frank. It had a horn handle and brown shaft and seemed quite ordinary, except for its weight, which was more than I had expected. My cousin unscrewed the handle from the shaft, and concealed internally was a recess in the handle for the placement of a cartridge, a trigger and cocking mechanism and a hollow barrel in the shaft. I had never seen one before. I took it to one of the leading national dealers in antique and modern guns, and after examining it, he gave me its history. Around the turn of the 20th century, gunsticks were common and were available in many catalogues. They were commonly carried by gentlemen as a form of protection against robbery. The gunsticks varied greatly in their decoration. The expensive and ornate gunsticks would be purchased by the *nouveau riche*, whereas those that were simple would be owned by old money, well-established upper class, and those less well off. The only decoration on my grandfather's cane was a ring of German silver. The appraiser estimated that my grandfather's gun stick was made between 1903–08 probably in Belgium.

Aunt Lena told me that Frank, early in his career as an artist, had a wealthy patron called Clifton Talbot, who was a well-known collector of rare orchids and lived at Liverpool. The Talbots invited Frank and Sarah to spend a weekend with them. The Wasleys had not been told that the Talbots had arranged a large reception for them. Everyone was wearing formal dress except the Wasleys, who felt embarrassed and humiliated. It must have hurt them especially because of the somewhat precarious hold that they felt they had on their social status. It might be expected that after Frank became a recognized artist he would grow less concerned about social class. Apparently, this did not happen. Later, when his elder daughter, Mary, married a farm labourer whom she had met when he was in the army in World War One, he ostracized her for marrying below her station. He did not see her again, or any of his grandchildren from that marriage. Frank did not appear to have a strong interest in the sales and promotion of his art.

My grandfather was tall, handsome and distinguished in appearance. He had a slim figure which he kept throughout his life, and dark hair. His younger daughters remembered him as serene, even-tempered, self-contained and quiet. Lena said that he was very much a ladies' man. Aunt Winifred once told her nephew, Jonathan, that Frank was sitting with a group of his men friends, and at a certain point, pulled a handkerchief out of his pocket. Instead of a handkerchief it was a paint rag – not surprising. But the paint rag was made of a pair of ladies' knickers – to the delight of Frank's friends.

Within a year of Frank and Sarah's marriage their first child, Mary Winifred, was born, and the following year my mother, Gladys, came along. A third daughter, Winifred, was born three years later. Mary's birth occurred at a village north of Manchester. Possibly the move there was to conceal the date of the birth. They then returned to Manchester, where the next two girls were born.

By this time, Frank had gained considerable recognition as an artist, his paintings appearing in a number of art galleries and exhibitions, including the Royal Academy. During the years when Frank and Sarah's three older children were growing up, Frank would have had a reasonable income.

Frank visited Whitby as early as 1890 and made it his home for three or more years around the turn of the century. It is easy to see why Frank was so attracted to the town. It is situated on the cliff-bound north-east coast of England at the mouth of the River Esk. Whitby's beginnings were in the seventh century, when Bede founded a religious house. In the following centuries, an abbey and monastery were built. It was sacked by the Danes, and for some time was a Danish colony. The ruins of the abbey still exist and stand on the east cliff, which dominates the harbour. It was a shipbuilding centre where the ship was built that was used by the famous explorer and navigator, Captain Cook, and it was an important port for fishing boats and coastal shipping. The harbour has a sea wall and lighthouse, and the old town of narrow streets stands on the steep slopes above the river.

The whole setting provided wonderful opportunities for a marine artist, and Frank took advantage of it with numerous paintings and charcoal drawing's. In searching for titles of Frank's art that include in their title, 'Whitby', I have found 13. The pictures include: a storm; trawlers caught in a gale; hauling in the catch; the cliffs; a scene from the river; the abbey; West Harbour with the mist rising; sailing boats; a ship in distress; and a wreck. There are other marine paintings which do not include the word 'Whitby', but may well have been painted there. While Frank was at Whitby, a laudatory article about his art was published in *The Artist* in 1901.

My mother would have been between about five and nine years old during the family stay in Whitby. In many parts of Britain the County Records Office have kept school records that go back as much as over a century. I wrote to the North Yorkshire office to see whether there was anything about the Wasley children. They found the following entry about Winifred, who was four years younger than my mother.

22 Nov. 1901. Winifred Wasley has made 12 attendances in the last four weeks.
29 Nov. 1901. Several children are still very irregular (in attendance), Winifred Wasley has been absent all the week, but on several occasions has been seen playing in the street.

In the limited search of the school records, this was all the records office found. Aunt Lena told me that her father took a casual view of formal education for girls, having become a successful artist without any formal training. He did send my mother and Mary to a convent boarding school, but this may have been motivated by religious concerns.

After the Wasleys left Whitby, I could learn nothing about the family until 1904, when the birth certificate of Lena, the youngest of the four girls, showed that they were living in Pangbourne, on the river Thames about 20 miles east of Oxford. With Frank's love of fishing and the beauty of the Thames, it is easy to see from the following description why Frank chose to come there. A brief description is given of the village in a booklet, *London's River, Father Thames, A Handbook for Those that Follow his Waterway*:

> At mile 13 we passed through Mapledurham lock and turned south west to Pangborne, mile 15, where there is a fine weir by the roadside much favored by fishermen with its pools and turbulent eddies.

A page of the booklet is devoted to angling.

> Angling is one of the most popular recreations on the Thames. The angling clubs are numerous and thousands of men and women come from far and wide for the pleasure of a day with a rod and line in some quiet beauty spot. That the Thames produces some fine fish there is abundant evidence to be found in the glass cases of the famous Angler's inns and it is in these riverside taverns that you will hear all the tales of the lovers of the sport.

Between 1904 and 1914 the family was on the move again, and I could find only fragments of evidence as to where they were. The photo of Frank sitting at his easel was taken at Stratford on Avon around 1908. Further evidence to suggest that they were living there comes from Barbara, my cousin, who lives in South Africa. She has a cup, won by her mother, Mary, at a regatta at Stratford on Avon. Titles of Frank's paintings around this period show a variety of sites in the same general area, and this suggests that the family may have continued to use short-term tenancies in rented houses.

In 1914, on the same day that Britain entered World War One, the Wasleys moved to Henley on Thames, where Frank and Sarah spent the remainder of their lives, except for a stay at Wargrave, a village upstream of Henley, where the Wasleys lived in a house someone lent to them. At this time Frank was 66 years old, and the daughters ranged in age from 23 to 10.

Lena's aunt had given her a piano which went with the family whenever it moved, and Frank played for several hours each day from printed music. Sarah had a good voice, and Frank often accompanied her. Sarah also played the piano, but for some reason Frank discouraged her from doing so. Lena recalled that there was little conversation at meals.

In Frank's landscapes, his frequent use of rivers may well have been influenced by his love of fishing. Lena remembered her father taking a punt out on the river and, when he found a scene that he liked, anchoring the punt, setting out his fishing rod and settling down to his painting. He also painted on the banks of rivers, and would take his fishing rod in hope of catching a fish. On one occasion, he had nearly completed a painting when he saw that there was a fish on his line. He left the painting to land the fish, and by the time he got back, found that cows that were grazing nearby had licked the paint off the canvas. Periodically, Frank would go off north by himself for salmon fishing.

Religion played a part in Frank's life, and he regularly attended mass as a Roman Catholic. When they were living at Wargrave, Frank walked several miles every Sunday to attend church at Henley. He went on his own, and Lena did not indicate that Sarah was a regular church attender. At one time Lena told me that her mother hated priests, but she could give no reason for this.

A mutual interest of Frank and Sarah was dogs. In photographs Frank is shown on a country walk with a small dog, and Frank and Sarah are portrayed with a large St Bernard called Pearl. There are several photos of the family taken in front of a haystack, at the time of Lena's twenty-first birthday. In each, a dog is included and is generally held by my mother. On one occasion, Pearl, who was large and strong, pulled Sarah off her feet and the fall broke her hip. Later, Pearl was partly responsible for Sarah's death. She was out with her elderly dog when he collapsed on the ground. It was raining, and Sarah held her umbrella over the dog until someone came along and went for help. Sarah got cold and wet while waiting, and this led to a cold which developed into pneumonia, from which she died.

Lena recalled that in the evenings, her father generally went out to the Conservative Club rather than stay at home. Even after Sarah broke her hip and was slowly recovering, he still retained this practice.

After the Wasleys came to Henley, lack of money became an increasingly pressing problem. It is likely that because of World War One the purchases of contemporary art declined steeply, and Frank had difficulty in selling his work. He was also ageing, and his output of art work may have declined. All the girls got jobs as soon as they left school, and Winifred and Lena (and probably the other sisters) gave part of their income to help support their parents. Lena remembered that her father could not afford school fees for her and gave art lessons at her school instead of fees. Frank received some help from a benevolent society that provided help for indigent gentlemen, and some organization helped pay for some of Lena's school tuition.

I am afraid that, despite my efforts to piece together what I could about my mother during her childhood, she still remains a shadowy figure. One can infer that she was limited in her experiences and remained somewhat naïve about the ways of the world. Her closest attachment was to her older sister, with whom she shared the experiences of a Catholic convent boarding school. Her parents, for different reasons, appeared to have had little time to spend with their daughters, and it must have been difficult for my mother to have bridged the eleven-year gap between her and her youngest sister. Because of this gap, Lena had few memories of my mother. Lena and Winifred spoke fondly of my mother, saying that she was a kind, gentle person, that she had a way with animals and was very fond of them, that she was passive and easily led. As we shall see, the four girls followed very different life paths after leaving school.

12

The Adult Lives of My Mother's Sisters

In this chapter, I will put down what I have been able to learn about my mother's three sisters as adults, and in the next chapter what I learned about my mother.

Mary

What I have learned about Mary comes from her daughter, Barbara, her youngest son, Peter, Aunt Lena and Walter Mason. As a young woman, the Wasley family expected that Mary would marry a solicitor, but after a row with her parents, Mary called off the wedding and left to train as a nurse. At the hospital, she worked with mentally ill patients and became engaged to a doctor who was German. When World War One seemed imminent, he was sent back to Germany, and she lost touch with him. I know nothing about her wartime work as a nurse, but gained some understanding of what it might have been like reading Vera Brittain's experiences of being a wartime nurse at that time in her book, *Testament of Youth*.

Brittain describes her work in London after one of the major battles of the war.

On that morning, July 4th, began the immense convoys which came without cessation for about a fortnight, and continued at short intervals for the whole of that sultry month and the first part of August. Throughout those 'busy and strenuous days' the wards sweltered beneath the roofs of corrugated iron; the prevailing odour of wounds lingered perpetually in our nostrils, the red-hot hardness of paths and pavements burnt its way through the soles of our shoes. Day after day I had to fight the queer, frightening sensation – to which, throughout my years of nursing, I never became accustomed – of seeing the covered stretchers come in, one after another, without knowing until I ran with pounding heart to look, what fearful sight or sound or stench, what problem of agony or immediate death, each brown blanket concealed. (pp. 279–280).

Brittain's working hours were from 7.45 a.m. until 1.00 p.m. and again from 5.00 p.m. until 9.15 p.m. When emergencies occurred the hours were far longer.

It is reasonable to think that some of Mary's and Vera Brittain's experiences were similar. In 1917, Mary met Walter Mason, a patient who was an Army Private, and in October the same year they were married. After the war ended, they moved to Skipton, Yorkshire, to the address given on my birth certificate, and Walter returned to his previous work as a farmer. To supplement her husband's income, Mary embroidered camisoles. I have told earlier about my mother's and my visit in 1920. In 1921, their first son was born and they moved to a farm near Skipton.

Walter and Mary had six children who survived and twin boys that died.

Shortly after, they rented and worked a farm called Higher Verges, up in the hills some miles away from Skipton. It had only one upstairs and one downstairs room with attached farm buildings. As the family grew, in 1936 they moved to a farm called Lower Verges that was nearby and had more living space. When the children were school age they had to walk five miles through the fields to their school. They all worked on the farm during the summer holidays, the only respite from this work being a one-day holiday when they went to Blackpool, a famous holiday resort on the north-west coast of England. Every Sunday Mary took the children to the Roman Catholic church, but Walter, who was not Catholic, did not attend.

The farm had no electricity and Mary did all the family wash, carrying the water from a well in the yard and doing all the work by hand. She baked bread for the family and made clothes for the children from secondhand clothes that she found and altered. She also worked on the farm. The never-ending work of the farm, housekeeping, childbearing and looking after her growing family must have been a hard life for Mary, and in striking contast to her parents' lifestyle when she was growing up.

At the beginning of World War Two the government stipulated what farmers could and could not do. Walter Mason did not like the government intervention, and left the farm because of this and moved to Earby, a nearby village. Unable to find work as a farmer, Walter joined the army and went to serve in France. From there he was sent to a hospital in England, suffering from rheumatoid arthritis, and it was several months before he was discharged from the army. After coming home, he was sent to a munitions factory where he did security work. The children were growing up, and eventually all of them joined the armed forces and moved away. At Earby there was a mill which was converted into a munitions factory during the war. Because of the housing shortage, the government ordered any householder who had any spare rooms to take in boarders. Mary complied by taking in four boarders from the factory. To help the family income, Peter, the youngest son, worked on a farm every summer from the age of ten. Trying to do the work of a man he felt led to the back troubles he experienced when he was older.

Mary's aunt, after whom she was named, lived in Bristol and was headmistress of a school. She was disabled with arthritis and needed help in her daily living. For years, this help had been supplied by a maid and by a man who acted as her chauffeur. Then the chauffeur was conscripted into war service and the maid left and could not be replaced.

Aunt Mary of Bristol wrote to her niece, Mary, asking her to come to Bristol to help her as housekeeper and companion, and in exchange she would receive the house after the older Mary died. Mary accepted, taking with her to Bristol her three youngest children. Peter only remained in Bristol for three weeks before returning to Yorkshire to work on a farm, and the two other boys joined the services as soon as they were old enough. Mary stayed with her aunt until she died, but for some reason did not inherit the house. Mary then did similar work for her other aunt, Nellie, who also lived in Bristol. Neither of the aunts were easy to get along with, and to gain some privacy and independence she moved to a flat of her own. After her second aunt died, Mary took jobs as companion to elderly ladies. Mary's husband had a job as nightwatchman and used to visit Mary at weekends. Walter became an alcoholic, and Mary refused to see him any longer, and later obtained a divorce. At one time, Walter became seriously ill and Mary went and nursed him. Mary lived in Bristol for nearly 20 years before a major change occurred in her life.

Brian, one of Mary's sons, was teaching at the Slade Art School in London and got to know George Byfield, one of the men employed as a model for the students. He was elderly and had very striking features, which made him a good model. Brian found him to be a well-educated gentleman, a widower, retired accountant and company secretary. Brian told his mother about him and arranged a meeting between them. George was very kind to Mary, they got along well together and decided to get married, which they did in 1963 at Harrow, north London. Mary was 71 years old and George was 84. Their marriage, according to their children, was a very happy one and lasted nine years until George's death. Mary could have stayed on at the house in Harrow, but George's son from his first marriage, who was co-executor of the estate, made her feel so uncomfortable that Mary went back to her youngest son, Peter, in Bristol. At that time Peter and his wife, Pauline, had a vegetable shop with a flat on the

88

second floor, and Mary moved in there. After Peter sold the shop they all moved into a cottage. This proved to be cold and damp in the winter, so Mary got a job as companion to an elderly lady who had a pleasant house with central heating, which was very comfortable in winter. Peter and Pauline made arrangements for Mary to move into a flat designed for elderly people, but before she could move in, Mary died in 1974 at the age of 82.

As far as I can determine, Mary never saw her parents after her first marriage, and Frank and Sarah never saw any of Walter and Mary's children. She was visited by Lena, and by my mother.

Winifred

Winifred was four years younger than my mother, and I learned about her adult life from Aunt Lena and Winifred's photograph albums, which provided a view of her life between the two world wars. Many of the photos were of her family, and all were neatly captioned with dates, showing a strong sense of organization. In her pictures, she appears self-assured and often smiling or laughing, whereas the others in the family seem more serious and, in the case of my mother, sometimes sad. There is a photo of Winifred standing in a narrow rowing boat, with one arm akimbo and the other proudly holding an upended oar. She is wearing a long, white dress with a sash around her waist and a necklace (see Fig 14). Throughout the albums there is not a single photo of Mary. This is further evidence of the ostracism of Mary following her marriage.

Winifred was 17 at the outbreak of World War One and I was unable to find out what she did during those war years. Afterwards, her height and striking appearance enabled her to get a job in one of the foremost modelling agencies, Enos of London. The models received many invitations to parties at the homes of wealthy, and some of the models married people they met at these gatherings.

Winifred attended these parties and made many friends among the models. They used to go on holidays together, both in Britain and on the continent.

I have a portrait of her taken from a magazine with the caption, 'Miss Winifred Wasley, who is playing the part of "Juliska" in *The Gypsy Princess* at the Prince of Wales Theatre. She is the daughter of well-known artist Frank Wasley of Wargrave, whose pictures of the Thames are popular.' In the portrait, she appears to be in her early twenties. She may well have had other acting and singing roles. Winifred had a talent for dressmaking and design, and later she worked for a clothes designer. I have a publicity studio portrait of her wearing a black dress and gloves, a hat and silver fox fur. Judging from her appearance and the fashion style, this was probably taken in the 1930s, when she was in her forties. By this time she had a flat in London and had bought an old double-decker bus that she converted into a holiday residence on the south coast at Selsey.

Winifred kept in touch with her family. Her photos in her album show pictures of family get-togethers, and she gave financial help to her parents when Frank no longer had any income. After my mother died and my half-sister Margaret was sent to a Catholic convent school, there is a picture of her and Lena taking Margaret out to a tearoom (see Fig 15). The two sisters paid Margaret's fees at the convent. After Sarah died in 1933, Frank lived with Lena, and then Winifred took him into her flat in London and cared for him until his death in 1934, aged 86.

At the outbreak of World War Two, Winifred, at the age of 42, went to work in an aircraft factory at Slough, near London. She found lodgings in the large house of a wealthy woman, and developed a long-term friendship with a woman staying at the same house. In her spare time, she often visited her sister, Lena, and her family, who lived nearby. Lena's son, Jonathan, remembers that on her visits she would bring him presents, and this was especially memorable because his parents did not give him presents.

On these visits, Winifred met a number of wealthy people whom she kept up with after the war.

Winifred married Toby Folks when she was nearly 50. They had known each other for many years prior to their marriage. He had been married to someone with a long-term disability, and it was only after her death that they were free to marry. They moved to a flat overlooking the sea at Hove, near Brighton, where Winifred lived until she died. The living room of their flat had walls lined with pictures of racehorses, and they spent much of their time going to horse races. Toby worked for a wine importer, and his connections with racing people whom they often met at cocktail parties were helpful for his company's wine sales. Winifred loved playing bridge, which she frequently did in the company of a group of Russian emigrés. My meeting with her was shortly before she died.

Winifred differed from her sisters in her independence, having far more control over her life and becoming well-off through her own efforts. She seemed to greatly enjoy life and had great self-assurance. Like her sisters, she was kind and thoughtful to people. She played by the rules of social class etiquette. Lena and her son, Jonathan, said she was a social snob. Jonathan told me of an incident which gave an indication of Winifred's attitudes to conventions of morality held in her generation. He lent her a book by Harold Nicolson and Vita Sackville-West about Harold's mother. The book describes how the mother developed a passionate relationship with Virginia Woolf, and their leaving their husbands and running off to France. When Winifred returned the book to Jonathan when he visited her, the book had been wrapped in a plain brown paper cover to conceal the title of the book, as if it were as scabrous as the book *Lady Chatterley's Lover*. I deeply regret that I only had one meeting with Winifred. I described this earlier, and was struck by her affectionate acceptance of a nephew she did not know existed.

Lena

Lena was the youngest of the family by eight years, and continued to live with her parents at Henley for 15 years until her marriage. She said somewhat ruefully to me that she had always been treated by Winifred as her little sister, and Winifred continued to organize her throughout her life. She was the daughter who was closest to her parents during the years when they were experiencing economic hardship. She left school at the age of 13 for financial reasons, and found odd jobs as a nanny. A woman friend of the Wasleys had learned to drive a car as part of her work in World War One. After the war, she started a taxi service and taught Lena how to drive so that she might be able to help in her taxi business. Lena developed a reputation of being a fast driver and was called on when clients of the taxi service were in a hurry.

A young man invited Lena to row a boat with him up the Thames to Oxford, spending nights at inns on the way. This idea did not appeal to Lena's mother, who insisted on going with them, even though in general, she disliked boating. When Lena was 24 she first met Bernard Elliman, the man she was going to marry. He was on a punt on the river with another man, and were playing gramophone records. Their marriage took place a year later. Her wedding dress was made for her by her sister, Winifred. Her husband, Bernard Elliman, combined practicing law with running the family business of making liniments for horses and people. Their homes at Guildford, Cookham Dean and Botolph Claydon were all within commuting distance of Bernard's work.

Lena and Bernard had two children: a girl, Joanna, who enabled me to first meet her mother, and a son, Jonathan, who was a teacher and then lived with his mother in order to help and take care of her in the years before her death at the age of 91. Although Henley was near where the Ellimans lived at Cookham Dean, Lena never showed her children where her parents had lived. Jonathan suggested that her reason for doing so was that she was ashamed of her parents' poverty, which included moving to avoid creditors.

Aunt Lena told me a story of her one attempt to make contact with Aunt Mary's children. They learned that one of Mary's sons, Fred, had joined a Guards regiment and was stationed at Buckingham Palace, doing guard duty. Bernard arranged a meeting with Fred and later, in describing the meeting, told Lena that they could never introduce Fred to any of their friends because of his broad Yorkshire accent. They never saw him again.

Apparently Lena did not concur with her father in his ostracism of her sister Mary, and used to visit her in Bristol after Frank's death. After Lena's husband, Bernard, died, she continued to live at the village of Botolph Claydon, where she had few friends. She was not part of the social life of the dominant Church of England, being a Catholic. The village was within commuting distance of London and its environs, and most of the residents were away during the day. She explained that the people up the hill were too upper-class to associate with her, while the villagers thought of her as too 'stuck up'. Her loneliness was mitigated by the presence of her son, Jonathan, who lived with her.

Before meeting Aunt Lena, I had been told by Aunt Winifred that Lena was a recluse and did not want to see me. As I found out, this was not true. Lena was glad to see me and was always kind and welcoming. I believe that Winifred's reasons for not wanting me to meet Lena were evident in her first letter to me in which she wrote, 'Lena and I don't want any more – we feel we are so disinterested in our relatives that we would rather leave things as they are.' On two occasions, Aunt Lena behaved in a way that puzzled both Jonathan and myself. On both occasions, she was reminiscing when she suddenly stopped and said, 'I can't tell you that. It is a secret.' The first time that this happened, I guessed that the secret had to do with her father marrying a second time when his first wife was still alive, but the second time was after we had shared this information. Jonathan responded the second time by saying to his mother that surely whatever it was happened so long ago that there was no longer any need to maintain secrecy, but Lena insisted that she could not reveal the secret.

13

The Adult Life of My Mother

Of all the Wasley family, the adult history of my mother proved to be the most elusive, despite a major investment of my time in the search. In this chapter, what I want to be prominent is what I could learn and surmise about my mother, so I will spare the reader much of the detail about how I gathered the information.

From the time that my mother left the convent boarding school around 1908, when she was 15 years old, until she became pregnant with me in 1919, my only direct source about her history came from Aunt Lena. She told me that my mother had two employers: Mr Clark, who was the head of a family business that manufactured various toilet preparations, and Mr Moyle, an eminent retired lawyer and widower. It is likely that she started her employment at an early age because her father was experiencing financial difficulties and would have been unable to support her.

The nature of her work is suggested by the occupation of 'Nurse Domestic' that she gave on my birth certificate. For a long time I assumed that this term was equivalent to a nanny who cared for children, and only later found out that it encompassed living with a family and caring for someone in the household. Because the Wasley parents were friends with both of her employers and they both had homes at North End, near Henley where the Wasley parents lived, it is probable that it was through them that she found the jobs. Mr Clark's main residence was in London, and his holiday home was in North End. He was elderly, with grown-up children, and he died shortly after my mother worked for him.

Aunt Lena recalled that in 1919 my mother moved to Cromer, she thought, to start another job. Cromer is a small holiday resort on the north shore of Norfolk. This move of my mother may well have been the result of finding that she was pregnant with me, and choosing to go somewhere remote from her family so that she could keep her pregnancy secret. I wondered how my mother would react to learning that she was going to have a child out of wedlock after attending a Catholic Convent boarding school, where she would have been given much instruction in the doctrines of the church. I asked my cousin Jonathan about this, since he had experienced a Catholic upbringing. He wrote as follows:

The approach of a religious community school would have been to indoctrinate the youngster through the Catechism, a standard list of questions and answers on matters of required knowledge and belief, often to be learned by heart; then frequent participation in the sacraments of mass, communion and confession.... In the catechism, non-standard behaviour is described as sin which can be venal (slight), or mortal (serious). The effect of being in a state of mortal sin is to be ineligible to take communion, to have had all grace (i.e. Brownie Points) removed, to have guilt; and this can be removed by going to confession. As all sexual behaviour outside of marriage is clarified as mortal sin, most young Catholics until recently lived in a state of constant anxiety, or partially, or completely left the church. Heavy-duty stuff, and another pall to weigh heavily on the social ease of someone like Gladys.

Her willingness to have me adopted by a non-sectarian, rather than a Catholic, agency suggests that she did not maintain close ties with the Catholic church, and these may have been loosened by the way the church treated her as an unmarried mother. If she left the church and its teachings, this may have alleviated the feelings of sin and guilt that a devout Catholic would have felt.

I made some enquiries at Cromer to try and find out what it would have been like for my mother during her stay there. An elderly woman told me a story to illustrate how unwed mothers were regarded around 1920. She had an aunt who was raised in a family in a small nearby town. The aunt's eldest sister used to go to work during the week and was always very well-dressed. Among her sisters she had always felt particularly close to the eldest. When she was in her teens, her father called her into his study and told her there was something that she ought to know. He and his wife were not her parents, but rather her grandparents, and her mother was actually the person whom she had always known as her eldest sister. When she was about 16, her mother married and wanted her daughter to come and live with her, but the grandparents were adamant in their refusal.

Dr Paul Barklay, an elderly retired physician who had always practised in Cromer, and whom I visited, felt that around 1920, the general view of a pregnant unmarried woman was moralistic, punitive and stigmatizing, but that some people, and many doctors, would have been understanding, kind, and helpful. He believed that my mother would have been able to find lodgings with a landlady who would have been kind and supportive, and a job in a hotel or guest house, for at that time there was a local shortage of help.

Although my birth certificate gave Skipton as my place of birth, what I had learned in my visit there (see Chapter 2) led me to conclude that I had been born elsewhere and then taken to Skipton, where my mother had registered the birth. At that time any record-keeping about births was very casual, and this would have been to my mother's advantage. There were a number of homes for unwed mothers where they could stay prior to and during the birth of their child. I had thought it possible that my

97

mother might have gone to one of these homes, and hoped to find one at, or near, Cromer. These homes kept records, and from them I might learn something about my parents. A list of the homes was in the *Charities Register*, where I had looked for adoption agencies. The homes were listed under a section entitled 'Penitents'.

The following descriptions of some of these agencies illustrate the severe stigma attached to unmarried mothers. 'For the shelter and reformation of girls who though fallen, are not sunk deeply in sin, but are anxious to redeem their characters and give promise of amendment of life.' At an orphanage the only children accepted were those who had been 'lawfully begotten'. In another home for young women and children, they accepted 'fallen women under 25' and 'unfallen women in circumstances of danger'. The former were to be kept apart from the latter. At a maternity home, only 'first fallen cases' were received. Not all of the agencies adopted this moralistic tone in their description. For example, an organization, 'Friends of Children', gave as their purpose, 'To encourage young mothers of illegitimate children to realize their responsibilities toward, and to assist them in the care and upbringing of such children.'

There were no homes listed in the vicinity of Cromer, and in one way I was glad that my mother probably did not go to such homes with the humiliation she might have suffered. It was most likely that my mother had a domiciliary delivery, unless she had experienced some complication that required a hospital delivery.

In Chapter 2, I described what I had learned about my mother, aged 27, during her brief visit to Skipton with me as a newborn child. The next time that I could locate my mother was at Cressy Towers, the adoption home in London of the National Children Adoption Association on the day that my guardianship was transferred from my birth mother to my adoptive mother. The evidence for this meeting comes from the document signed by both parties on 18 April 1921. How long I was with my birth mother before she took me to the adoption agency, and where she lived, I do not know. At the adoption, my birth mother gives her parents' address. She could have returned to their home by this time and retained the secret of my birth because there would be no evidence in my mother's appearance of what had happened.

I tried to imagine the emotionally charged scene at the adoption agency in which the indenture was signed by the two parties to the agreement in the presence of two witnesses. I feel that it must have been a very hard and sad experience for my birth mother, and that the joy my adoptive mother probably felt was tempered by her awareness of what the occasion meant for my birth mother. The signature of my adoptive mother I immediately recognized, having seen it countless times, but it was the first time that I had seen the neat, clear signature of my birth mother. I wondered what a handwriting expert would read into that signature. After stating the names of the two parties to the agreement, the indenture reads 'Whereas the mother of an illegitimate child known as Francis Sydney Wasley...'. Although probably unintentionally so, the use of the term 'illegitimate' seems unnecessarily cruel when the word had so many negative and stigmatizing connotations, and could have easily been omitted. The name of the witness to my birth mother's signature was already familiar to me. It was Frank Moyle, the eminent lawyer for whom my mother had been housekeeper shortly before she became pregnant with me. My mother must have turned to him for help some time before or after my birth, feeling that she could trust him to keep her secret. He probably played an important role in arranging for the adoption. The person who was the witness to my adoptive mother was unknown to me.

Only after writing this chapter did I find out how different my subsequent life might have been. Margaret Humphreys, author of a book, *Empty Cradles*, brings to light the generally unknown history of the export of British children to the colonies, especially Canada and Australia. I could easily have been one of these children. The rationale for sending the children was two-fold: the countries to which they were sent needed more people to increase sparsely populated areas, and it was cheaper to send children than adults. From the viewpoint of the British government and of the different agencies that ran homes for children, the export of children provided a way of dealing with the problems of overcrowding that existed in many of the child agency homes. The child migration schemes 'involved virtually all the major child care agencies and charities in the UK – Dr Barnardo's, the National Children's Home, the Fairbridge Society, the Salvation Army, Quarrier Homes – and a variety of social welfare agencies operating under the umbrellas of the Catholic Church, the Church of England, the Presbyterian Church and the Church of Scotland.' (p.79) Some new agencies were formed especially to promote child migration.

Between 1880 and about 1930, over 100,000 children were sent to Canada. As this stream of migration diminished, the stream to Australia increased. Between 1924 and 1940, 1,225 children were sent to Australia. The child migration was subsidized by both the British and the host countries. The benefits for the children were given as 'rescuing them from difficult conditions for the greater good of themselves and the Empire.' (p.80). 'The reasoning was simple enough. As victims of poverty or broken homes, these children were regarded as "deprived" and considered a burden on society... similarly they would grow up to be thieves and hooligans and probably finish up in jail. Already this urban flotsam was filling orphanages and poor houses.... Children could be rescued from vice and deprivation and be sent to populate the Empire and its Dominions, where fresh air, hard work and religious instruction would make them fine, upstanding citizens.'

What had been neglected in this large-scale social engineering was a concern for the welfare of the children and what the effects would be on their lives. An investigation of the children's lives by Margaret Humphreys found that many of the children had, on arrival in Australia, been placed in institutions where conditions were frequently appalling. Children were physically and sexually abused, used as unpaid labour, isolated from any community and starved of any affection. Their experiences left lifetime emotional and social problems, yet this remained largely unknown to both the Australian and British publics until uncovered by Margaret Humphreys.

My mother could easily unwittingly have given me to a child agency that would have sent me abroad without the permission or knowledge of my mother, and if she had come back to reclaim me, she could have been told, as some mothers were, that I had either been adopted, or had died. Thanks to the way that Frank Moyle guided my mother through the adoption process, I may have been spared from being deported.

There is another gap in time that I was unable to fill in, from early 1921 to 1923. In Aunt Winifred's photo albums there are several photos of my mother taken at her parents' home and in the garden. One is of my mother with Winifred and Lena wearing summer dresses and large hats taken by the Thames at Henley (see Fig 16). Several were taken with a haystack as background, and in all of them my mother is holding a dog, or a cat. One picture shows my mother with her father and Lena on a country walk. She is alone only in one photo, taken of her standing by the fireside in her parents' house. Aunt Lena remembers my mother returning to her parents to nurse her mother after she had broken her hip, the break being caused by Sarah's large dog knocking her over.

In 1923–24 my mother went to work at Courtlands, a model farm, at Horsham, Sussex, south of London. I can see her there in three photos. In one she is standing in front of some cows and carries a milking stool and pail (see Fig 17); in another she is holding a nanny goat with one hand and a baby goat with the other, and the last shows her standing and holding the head of a cow. It is clear that my mother

101

had a great affection for animals. While on the farm, she continued visiting her parents' as some 1925 photos show.

While at the farm she got to know her future husband, Bernard Mahon. He was one of ten children of Irish Catholic parents. After leaving school he passed a civil service examination and was placed in a job that bored him. He left the job and went to South America, where he worked in a bank in Buenos Aires. When World War One started, Bernard came back to Britain, joined a Scottish regiment and served in France. At the end of the war he returned to South America and took up his work again in a bank. He contracted malaria and was advised by a doctor to return to England and get a job working outdoors. This he did, choosing Courtland farm. The source of my information about Bernard Mahon was his second wife, whom he married after the death of my mother.

In January 1926, my mother married Bernard Mahon at a registry office in the District of Camberwell in South London. Bernard was 40 and Gladys was 32. Bernard's occupation was given as 'Chauffeur Domestic', his condition 'Bachelor' and his residence in Herne Hill in London. Gladys gave no occupation, her parents' address and her father's occupation as landscape painter. Aunt Lena was one of the witnesses, but had no recollection of the event. Neither of my grandparents was present, in contrast to Lena's wedding, which was a large, formal church wedding. Four months after my mother's wedding, my half-sister, Margaret, was born, and this may have accounted for the choice of a registry office marriage and the absence of Gladys' parents. Her marriage to a chauffeur may have also led to her being ostracized by her father, the second daughter to marry below her station. Neither the two younger daughters made this mistake. Margaret's birth was registered at Reigate, Surrey, and the parents gave separate addresses in London. To what extent the decision to marry was influenced by my mother's pregnancy I do not know, but if it was the primary reason it must have been a very hard decision for my mother. Six years earlier she had

102

given me up for adoption and, possibly, she could not face once more having a child out of wedlock and again having to give it up.

My mother had only seven years of married life left before she died, and during this time she had no home of her own and lived sometimes with her husband and sometimes on her own as domestic help in rooms in her employers' houses. The only specific information I was able to find out about her life was a two-year period when she and her husband were employed by Viscount and Lady Maugham at their country estate south of London. The clues that led to this information were photographs my half-sister had kept of herself as a small child. Some showed her in a large, well-tended garden with an imposing brick house in the background. On the back of one of them was written 'Hartfield' and on another, 'Tye House'.

After locating the village and house, I found, through the county voting registers, that the occupants of Tye House were Sir Frederick Maugham and Lady Helen Maugham, and for 1929 and 1930 the names of my mother and her husband were also given. I found in *Debrett's Peerage* that one of the Maugham's daughters lived in London, and wrote to her explaining who I was and asking whether she had any memories of my mother. She replied, 'It will not be easy, as you may surmise, because there were so many people coming and going at Tye House. It was long ago and I was a heedless girl at the time, full of my own affairs, not noticing much unless it concerned me directly.' She would talk to her elder sister, but felt that the most likely source of information about my mother was her mother's diaries, which she had in her possession. I was touched by the friendliness of the letter and by the charming assessment of herself as a girl.

In her next letter, Mrs Marr Johnson enclosed extracts from her mother's diaries which were largely about her family, but made some references to my mother and her husband. In her letter she wrote that in reading her mother's diaries she remembered how much her mother had liked my mother and her husband. I had told her that my mother had died of cancer in 1933, and in response to this she noted that the diaries established that my mother was well when she left Tye House late in 1929.

Reading her mother's diaries brought back to Mrs Marr-Johnson some memories which she shared with me in her letter. Her family had used Tye House only at weekends and holidays, and spent the rest of the time at a large house in Cadogan Square in London. At Tye House at weekends there were constant house parties, and the domestic staff from the London house were brought down to help. During the weekdays Tye House would be very quiet, and my mother would function as housekeeper. Mrs Johnson's mother 'so loved the peaceful times when she would stay during the week after all the guests had gone.' Although my mother's husband generally worked as a chauffeur he did not perform this role at Tye House, because the family already had a chauffeur, who had been with the family a long time and would have deeply resented anyone usurping his position.

Lady Maugham's diary extracts established the dates of the Mahons (my mother's married name) arrival and departure from Tye House: from 4 February 1928 to 1 February 1 1930. The Mahons did some of the cooking as shown by an entry, 'the kitchen maid is cooking for us as the Mahons have gone on holiday'. Bernard Mahon is mentioned several times: how he helped put out a fire when some burning wood fell out of the fireplace and set the rug on fire; how he reported that he had seen three cubs in the den below the house, and his report of unusually heavy rain; how he reported that... 'they were using too much water and I have had to cut off all baths'. After the Mahons had been at Tye House for a week there is an entry, 'The new couple, the Mahons, seem very nice and quite excellent'. Mention is made of the Mahons going on holiday, and on another occasion, 'the Mahons have friends for Christmas and are not going for a holiday'. 'Spent a very happy and peaceful day with only the

Mahons to look after us'. 'Mahons bought a darling sheepdog puppy to keep here'. 'Little Peggy Mahon has a rash and the doctor does not know what it is. I hope it is not any disease'. When the Maughams' son was visiting them at Tye House he brought some films that he showed to the Mahons and the other domestic staff. These diary entries are tantalizingly brief, but do provide a fleeting glimpse of what the lives of the Mahons must have been like at Tye House.

The end of the Mahons' stay is shown in Lady Maugham's diaries on 15 January: 'I wrote to the Mahons at Tye House and said I must economize in the house, and that they had better look for another place'. On 18 January: 'I had a long talk with the Mahons who will go when they get a place to suit them'. 31 January: 'The Mahons leave today to go to a Mrs Lucker'.

Diana Marr Johnson asked me to visit her if ever I came to London, and I accepted the invitation. Her flat had a balcony overlooking a spacious garden surrounded by several large five-storey white houses. After lunch, Diana showed me an album of photographs taken at Tye House about the time my mother had been there. Most of the pictures were of three to six young adults taken during weekend or summer visits. Some showed young men and boys on horseback, the farm which was on the grounds of Tye House and the farmer, whom she said was dishonest. She had found two photos of my half-sister, Peggy, taken in front of well-kept flowerbeds in the garden. Diana told me that the family were very upset when her father bought Tye House, because they already had a country house near Bath which they greatly preferred to Tye. Her father gave as his reason for his decision that it was far closer to their London House. When Diana was at Tye she used to play golf and tennis, went for walks and played indoor games. I learned little more about my mother at Tye, but Diana told me something about her mother's life at their London house. After breakfast every day, she and the cook made out the day's menus. Harrods called at an agreed upon time every morning, took the order, and it was delivered shortly afterwards. The time passed only too quickly during my visit with Diana, and I greatly enjoyed meeting her.

I later learned that the Maughams' son, Robin, had written two autobiographical books, and I read both. He devoted considerable space to describing his uncle, Somerset Maugham, the author, whom he greatly liked. Of his parents, he wrote, 'When we were young we were largely compensated for our father's remoteness by our mother's affection and all four of us adored her'. 'My father was quiet, dignified, reserved and solemn; my mother was irresponsible, cheerful and high-spirited'. In another place, he quoted what Cyril Asquith had written about his mother '...she had the secret of disengaging the kernel of fun or absurdity which often lurks within the most unpromising material and bringing it to the surface, a process warming the cockles of the heart and of the mind. It was this along with her unforced unposed appearance to people and things that made her one of the happiest human beings and a potent and persuasive cause of happiness to others. In her presence shyness was disarmed, diffidence melted, spirits rose, dullness began to emit sparks, or think it was doing so, while the most exacting were held, charmed and exhilarated'. These descriptions suggest that my mother and her husband were fortunate to have worked for Lady Maugham.

My sister Margaret also had some other photos taken of her at Tye House. In one, our mother is lying on her back with her arms outstretched, dangling Margaret, who was about two. In another, our mother is kneeling with her arm around Margaret, with a fox terrier sitting beside them. Our mother is wearing a housekeeping apron (see Fig 18). There also a photo of Margaret sitting on Aunt Lena's knee, so our mother must have had some contact with Lena around her time at Tye House.

There remained less than three years of my mother's working life after leaving Tye House and going to Mrs

Luckers before the development of cancer led to her entry into St Thomas' Hospital in London. During this period, the only clue I found about a place of employment was under the heading 'Occupation' on her death certificate. It read 'Of Manor Cottages, Shepherds Lane, Hurley, Berkshire'. The information was supplied by my mother's husband, who gave a separate address in London.

The address was part of a property owned by Lady Irene Vanbrugh, a famous actress, and it is a reasonable assumption that my mother worked for her. Despite various efforts, I was unable to find anyone who had any memories of my mother.

Aunt Lena remembered that when my mother was beginning to ail with cancer, she returned to her parents' home. This must have been shortly before my mother was hospitalized at St Thomas' Hospital. They transferred my mother to St Joseph's Hospice on 10 April 1933, where she died three months later at the age of 39. The death certificate gave as the cause of death: 'a) Morbis Condis; b) Metastases; c) Carcinoma of stomach'. There was no post-mortem. The hospice was well-regarded as a pioneer in its field. My half-sister, Margaret, recalled that she had ridden on the back of her father's motorcycle to visit our mother at the hospice, and our mother had said to her, 'All I want to do is to die.' I hope that my mother's last days at the hospice were not dominated by pain and that she was given support and comfort. We know that she was visited by her immediate family, Bernard and Margaret.

The photographs suggest that my mother found Margaret a great joy, but what about her relationship with her husband, and what sort of a person was he? I had learned that Sarah Wasley was outspoken in her dislike of Bernard, and that Lady Maugham had said positive things about him in her diary. The only other information about Bernard that I obtained was from Vera Mahon, his second wife. She told me that he strongly disliked children and had told her when they married that if she became pregnant he would walk out on her. They never had children, although she wanted them. He felt ill at ease with children and did not know how to handle them. She recalled that after their marriage, when Margaret as a teenager was living with them, he would yell at her about her table manners until Vera would remonstrate, but if Margaret did something really serious such as stealing he would just laugh it off and do nothing. Bernard's dislike of children may have been a source of friction between him and my mother. He was also very fond of gambling, and this could have led to difficulties.

My mother's married life was not easy, and I hope that she found some happiness during that time. Her life was cut off by cancer, so different from the long lives of her sisters. She seemed to let the currents that surrounded her move her through her life, rather than consciously directing her life toward goals that she set. She had a gift with animals, was kind and loving, with a calm temperament.

CONCLUSION

After 13 years of searching for my biological family many questions remain unanswered. A friend observed that I could continue searching for the rest of my life, but it was time to stop and focus instead on how and what I had learned. I have taken his advice. The resulting book is only part of what I have gained of value. When I began, my main motivations were curiosity and the challenge of trying to solve a mystery. But the search has been gratifying in other ways. It has taken me to many new and interesting places and enabled me to meet a wide variety of people. The relatives I have met have been generous in giving me information, their friendship and affection. From what I have learned of my heritage I have discovered much about myself and have developed strong emotional ties to my mother, aunts and grandparents. I feel singularly fortunate in being part of two families; the Richardsons and the Wasleys. I hope the readers of this book will share some of my excitement and feelings in this adventure.

AUTHOR'S NOTE

The Register of Births, Deaths and Marriages is no longer at St Catherine's House. It is now at the Family Records Centre, 1 Myddelton Street, London, EC1R 1UW.